# Chain Mail & Wire Reimagined

KAREN RAKOSKI
BARBARA DEYOUNG

KALMBACH BOOKS

**Kalmbach Books**
21027 Crossroads Circle
Waukesha, Wisconsin 53186
www.Kalmbach.com/Books

Published in 2015
19 18 17 16 15    1 2 3 4 5

Manufactured in the United States of America

ISBN: 978-1-62700-045-1
EISBN:978-1-62700-186-1


**Editor:** Erica Swanson
**Book Design:** Elizabeth Weber
**Illustrator:** Kellie Jaeger
**Photographers:** William Zuback, James Forbes


**Library of Congress Control Number:** 2014950468

# Contents

INTRODUCTION......................................................4

TOOLS & MATERIALS.........................................6

## THE PROJECTS
### LOOPS
Twine & Vines Bracelet Double Half Persian ..........................10
Trillium Flower Necklace Helm ...............................15
Caged Mail Pendant Helm Flower .........................20

### SINGLE WIRE
Hydrangea Bracelet European 4-in-1.....................24
Triple Twist Necklace Full Persian..........................28
Cleo's Charms Bracelet Helm ................................32
Shooting Stars Necklace Full Persian .....................36

### MULTIPLE WIRES
Draping with Daisies Necklace Helm Flower.............41
Rose and Thorns Bracelet Helm..............................45
Stars of the Sea Necklace Scallop...........................50
Valley Ferns Necklace Diagonal Byzantine ...............55

### FRAMES
Diamond Solitaire Necklace European 4-in-1 ...........61
Geometric Sliders Necklace Full Persian...................66
Three Wishes Necklace European 4-in-1 ..................70

### BRANCH AND WRAP
Spider Mums Bracelet Box Chain............................77
Squares and Lace Bracelet Victorian Lace.................80
Dragon Pillows Bracelet Dragonscale ......................86
Byzantine Waterfall Necklace Byzantine....................91

## TECHNIQUE REFERENCE
### CHAIN MAIL TECHNIQUES
Box Chain ...............................................................97
Byzantine ..............................................................97
Diagonal Byzantine ...............................................98
Double Half Persian................................................99
Dragonscale ..........................................................100
European 4-in-1......................................................101
Full Persian ...........................................................102
Helm......................................................................103
Helm Flower and Cleo's Helm................................104
Scallop...................................................................105
Victorian Lace........................................................106

### WIRE TECHNIQUES

FROM THE AUTHORS .................................110

# Introduction

When it comes to chain mail and wirework, we're both teachers, and our students have provided a few hints as to what they would like to see in a book. We took their suggestions to heart. Hopefully these designs and techniques will be "just what you wanted."

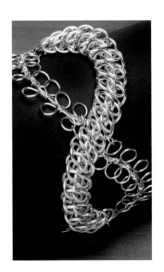

### MAKE A GOOD REFERENCE SOURCE

We are teachers to the core, plain and simple. An idea doesn't even have to have all the bugs worked out of it before we need to show someone where it is at and where it is going. Once the technique is refined and the directions make sense: class is in session! That is where you come in. These designs and techniques are ready for you. If you like to see everything step by step, it's here in text and pictures. The directions should help you make exactly what you see in the book. When you are ready to stretch what you see into the direction of your personal vision and designs, we have added some variations, concepts, and techniques to give you ideas.

### SHOW TECHNIQUES, NOT JUST PROJECTS

Perhaps you have had a lot of experience and were looking for a more challenging technique or two. Maybe bending your first piece of wire is ahead of you. Possibly the lines and designs of the jewelry in this book have caught your attention and you wish to make and wear them or give them as gifts. Or maybe you are able to peek a little into the future and can envision using the techniques and ideas to springboard your own work. Whatever paths led you here, we want to help provide opportunities, experiences, and creative directions that help you enjoy the processes and the results of playing with wire and jump rings.

## MAKE THE JEWELRY WEARABLE

Wire can tell a story, paint a picture, capture space, or make a connection. In many ways, the jump rings in chain mail are just fine wires with well-rounded personalities. Wire and chain mail also have some very different characteristics in drape, and density, and dimension. They are worn differently. They are shaped differently for functionality and comfort. The designs in this book came first. There was no way to make them with just wire or just chain mail. The combination is simply...magical.

## MAKE IT EASY AT FIRST—AND THEN MORE COMPLEX

The layout of this book follows the evolving designs made with wire. First, there is a single wire used in a simple formation. Then there are more wires and more complex formations. Each project includes the specific directions and materials for the variation of the basic chain mail pattern that will be required to make the piece shown. A technique reference in the back of the book will guide you through various techniques as needed; flip to this section for more detailed instructions for making wire shapes and chain mail weaves. You can pick out an easier project near the beginning of the book and beginning of each chapter, or you can just dive in and select your favorite.

## MAKE IT LOOK AMAZING

The designs in this book are meant to have the look of classic upscale jewelry. When you wear these pieces (and your personal variations) we want people to ask, "Where did you get that?" instead of "Did you make that?" Everyone deserves a little awe and amazement from their friends and fans.

The pieces are shown in a narrow color palette to emphasize the "look." The pieces are shown in enamel-coated copper wire or sterling for affordable style—but by all means, move up to silver and gold when you are comfortable with the techniques and have picked a favorite piece. The

pieces are all shown in bold and prominent size, which is also great for showing techniques and directions. Not everyone wears statement pieces, though, so we include some directions for going from delectable to delicate, as well as smaller design alternates if you don't feel like tackling a large necklace or bracelet.

## KEEP THE TOOLS AND MATERIALS BASIC

Considering that this book starts you on a journey toward fashion jewelry, you might expect special tools and devices. The truth is that sometimes a special pair of pliers or cutters will help you make the finished product more easily. So, when a specialty tool can make the job a bit easier, we will tell you about it. But remember, we were thinking about you—so every design in this book can be made with the most basic pliers, a cutter, a measuring device, and a few dowels.

## HELP ME WITH MY DESIGNS

Creativity comes with "stretch." After a technique is learned and mastered, and long after the favored pieces are made and being worn, we hope that the book will continue to offer you opportunities and ideas. Wirework and chain mail can continue to be a timeless springboard for your own designs and creative process.

Enjoy creating and playing with wire!

– Karen and Barbara

> When you wear these pieces, we want people to ask, "Where did you get that?"

# Tools & Materials

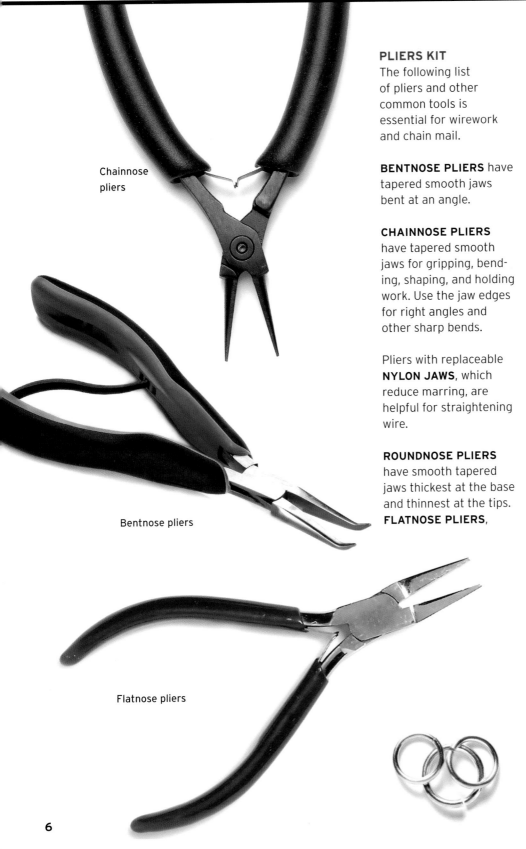

Chainnose pliers

Bentnose pliers

Flatnose pliers

**PLIERS KIT**
The following list of pliers and other common tools is essential for wirework and chain mail.

**BENTNOSE PLIERS** have tapered smooth jaws bent at an angle.

**CHAINNOSE PLIERS** have tapered smooth jaws for gripping, bending, shaping, and holding work. Use the jaw edges for right angles and other sharp bends.

Pliers with replaceable **NYLON JAWS**, which reduce marring, are helpful for straightening wire.

**ROUNDNOSE PLIERS** have smooth tapered jaws thickest at the base and thinnest at the tips. **FLATNOSE PLIERS,** with a flat, rectangular surface, are recommended for opening and holding jump rings, wires, wire bundles, and other flat work.

**FLUSH CUTTERS** slice wire cleanly without creating a tapered edge. "Razor-cut" pliers offer the best cut.

**OTHER HELPFUL TOOLS**
**DOWELS,** turned to specific dimensions, come in various sizes for making jump rings, coils, and repeatable bends.

Use a light adhesive **TAPE** that will not leave a residue (quilters tape) to secure wire bundles and mark measurement positions on pliers' jaws.

Both a straight-edge **RULER** and a **FLEXIBLE TAPE RULER** are helpful.

Use a **FINE-TIP PERMANENT MARKER.** Remove marks with denatured alcohol or **ACETONE**.

Keep your tools clean, in working order and sized for the appropriate gauges. Use **SAFETY GLASSES** when cutting.

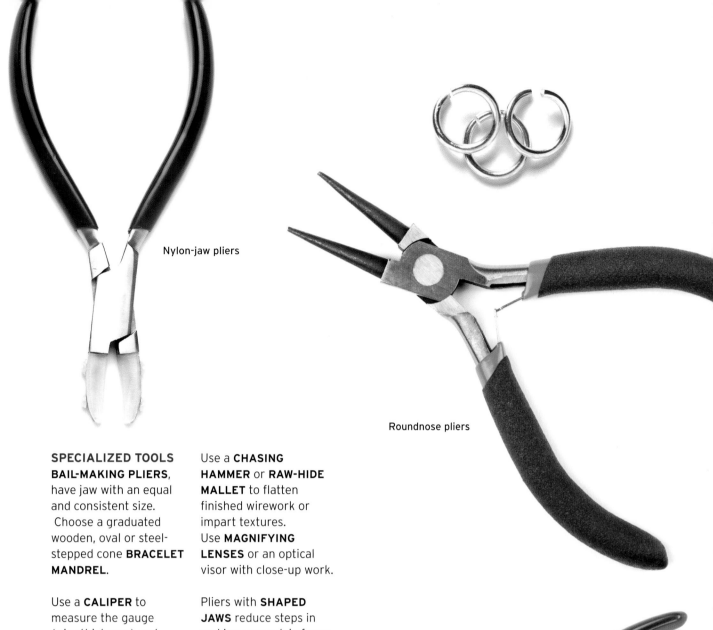

Nylon-jaw pliers

Roundnose pliers

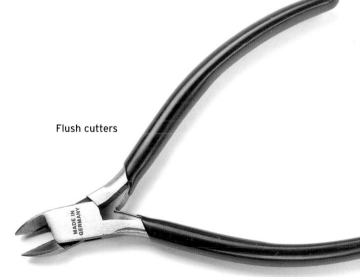

Flush cutters

**SPECIALIZED TOOLS**
**BAIL-MAKING PLIERS**, have jaw with an equal and consistent size. Choose a graduated wooden, oval or steel-stepped cone **BRACELET MANDREL**.

Use a **CALIPER** to measure the gauge (wire thickness) and inner diameter of chain mail jump rings and check wire sizes.

You can use a **COIL MAKER,** electric drills, hand-cranked tools, or even wooden dowels to wrap wire for different size coils. Use roundnose pliers' jaws for graduated coils.

Choose jewelry **FILES** to smooth wire ends and de-burr jump rings. **ACETONE** or denatured alcohol will remove wire marks and tape residue.

Use a **CHASING HAMMER** or **RAW-HIDE MALLET** to flatten finished wirework or impart textures.
Use **MAGNIFYING LENSES** or an optical visor with close-up work.

Pliers with **SHAPED JAWS** reduce steps in making geometric forms and also improve the consistency of edge size and the radius of bends.

Use a **RING OPENER**—a finger band with sized slots—to open jump rings with only one pair of pliers and without putting the chain mail down.

A hand-cranked **TUBE WRINGER** makes perfect, uniform, and wonderful waves in metals and wires.

Tumbling with a **TUMBLER**, a polishing technique for metal pieces, uses stainless steel shot and a burnishing liquid to polish and de-burr. (Tumbling is not recommended for enamel-coated copper.)

## MATERIALS

For most of the projects in this book, you won't need much beyond wire and jump rings.

**JUMP RINGS** used in chain mail are referenced by wire size (gauge), ring size (measured by inner diameter), and aspect ratio.

The gauge is the thickness of the wire. The larger the gauge is, the thinner the wire is. Most chain mail jewelry uses 14–20 gauge wire.

There are two common gauge standards: American (AWG) and British (SWG). The designs in this book use the AWG wire standard.

The inner diameter (ID) is the size of the hole inside the ring. That hole can be measured in inches or millimeters (mm). When ordering supplies for designs in this book, ask for IDs in millimeters. The inch equivalents do not always work the same.

Aspect ratio is the term that defines the relationship between gauge and inner diameter, and it is important when choosing rings for a particular chain mail weave. The "mathematical" definition of aspect ratio is inner diameter (ID) divided by wire gauge. But there is an easier way to understand it.

Using the example of an 18-gauge 4mm Byzantine weave, 18-gauge is the thickness of the wire, 4mm is the size of the hole inside the ring, and aspect ratio is the number of 18-gauge rings that can fit into a 4mm hole. Since 18-gauge wire is 1.0mm thick, four rings can fit into a 4mm hole, and the aspect ratio is four.

The same weave can use different wire gauges. The 16-gauge full Persian in the Triple Twist is bold and forceful, while the same weave with 20-gauge rings in the Geometric Sliders is diminutive and delicate. When you change gauge sizes for a particular weave, the ID must change with the same aspect ratio. Although the math for this change is precise, the ring size requirements for certain weaves may not always translate well from gauge to gauge. We recommend that you buy your rings in the sizes listed.

For the projects in this book, we use dead-soft **WIRE** (the softest wire) because the pieces require a lot of manipulation. Beginning with hard or half-hard wire makes wrapping multiple times difficult.

The wrapping wire sizes are generally 22- and 24-gauge, and "sewing" wire gauges are very fine (28- and 30-gauge).

18- or 21-gauge square and twisted square wire allow you to fabricate most shapes by hand. 18-gauge half-round wire is used for designs requiring structural support. Choose 21-gauge half-round wire for lighter binding or decorative wires.

# CHAPTER 1

# Loops

# Twines &Vines

This fun cuff-style bracelet is made with just three structural pieces. The vines of round sparkling leaves wind, curl, and intertwine with a band of shaped double half Persian silver. The chain mail hides the secret to retaining the bracelet's form: an almost invisible backbone of supportive 20-gauge wire. This gives the piece a wrist-hugging curve while keeping it adjustable for wearable comfort.

## MAKE THE CHAIN MAIL

**1** Make a 5" (13cm) piece of **double half Persian** chain mail using 6mm jump rings (p. 99).

## MAKE THE VINE WITH CLOSURE LOOP

**2** Cut a 36" (.9m) length of 20-gauge gold wire. Leaving a 1" (2.5cm) tail, begin wrapping the wire around the dowel to make 16 **side-by-side coil loops (photo a)**, keeping the continuous path even along the bottom.

**3** Make the turn by creating the next loop so its bottom touches loop 16, but is at a right angle to the first row of loops **(photo b)**. This newly formed loop

## MATERIALS

**wire**
- 72" (1.8m) 20-gauge, gold (36"/.9m for each vine)
- 6" (15cm) 20-gauge, silver
- 36" (.9m) 24-gauge, silver

**jump rings**
- **40** 6mm 16-gauge, silver
- **8** 3mm 20-gauge, gold

**tools**
- pliers kit
- ³⁄₁₆" (5mm) dowel
- permanent marker

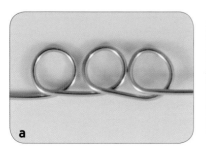

a

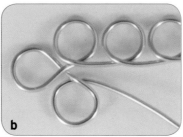

b

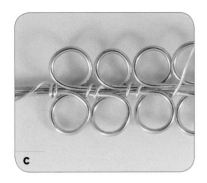

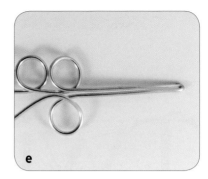

c

d

e

17 will be the closure loop once it is wrapped at the base.

**4** Make the turn again by creating the next coil loop so the bottom touches both the base of the closure loop and the bottom of loop 16 **(photo b, p. 11)**. Coil loop 18 will be the first loop of the second half of the vine. (The second set of loops faces away from the first set.)

**5** Match the continuous path for the next loops along the original base, and make a total of 16.

**6** Use 24-gauge silver wire for wrapping. Leaving a 1" tail, make two wraps at the point where the double rows of loops meet, ending with the wire in back of the work.

**7** Keep the two base paths flat, parallel, and close together. Keep the loop rows to the outside. Carefully position the loops in the initial row directly across from the loops in the second row. Move the wrapping wire to the space between the first and second set of round loops. Wrap the base path wires twice to join them, ending with the wire in the back. Repeat **(photo c)** until all 16 base path spaces are joined.

**8** Wrap the wrapping wire around the base of the single loop 2-4 times, ending with the wire at the back of the work. Trim the excess wire, and tuck the end in for a smooth finish **(photo d)**. Use the 24-gauge wire tail from step 6 to wrap the base wires three more times, ending at the back. Trim the wire and tuck the end. Using roundnose pliers, bend the tails of the base wires over the trimmed silver wire ends. Trim

the excess base wires just beyond the wire wraps. Use roundnose pliers to roll and tuck these ends toward the back of the vine so they are smooth.

Each vine and the silver band has an overall finished (curved) length dimension of 3½" (8.9cm).

## MAKE THE VINE WITH A CLOSURE HOOK

**9** Repeat step 2. Make an extension for the hook: ³/₄" (1.9cm) from the base of loop 16, use chainnose pliers to make a sharp bend and fold the wire back toward the base.

**10** Make a loop directly across from the loop in the initial row **(photo e)**. Repeat for a total of 16 loops. Keep the two base paths flat, parallel, and close together.

**11** Repeat steps 6-8, but wrap the base of the hook extension instead of the loop.

**12** Place the wrapped vine right side up. Use the wire extension created in step 9 to make a **clasp hook**.

## CURVE THE VINES

**13** Mark each vine at the quarter, half, and three-quarter marks.

f

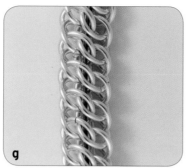

g

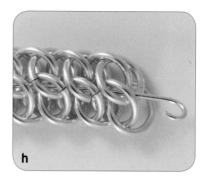

h

**14** Curve the vine with the closure loop: Face the loop to the left, and bend the left quarter-portion down. Make the highest point at the first quarter point. Curve/bend the main (right) part of the link down. Three quarters of the way along, curve the right end up even with the bottom of the first loop. Adjust the length of the piece with more or less curve until the span of the final piece is 3½" (8.9cm) **(photo f)**.

**15** Curve the vine with the hook: Face the hook to the right, and bend the left quarter edge down. Make the highest point at the first quarter. Curve/bend the main (right) part of the vine down. A quarter of the way from the end, curve the end up even with the bottom of the left edge. Adjust the length of the piece with more or less curve until the span of the final piece is 3½".

Both pieces will have identical curves. The loop will be on the left side facing down. The hook will be on the right side facing up.

**STIFFEN THE CHAIN MAIL**

**16** Cut a 6" (15cm) piece of 20-gauge wire, and make a small hook on one end. String the straight end of the wire through the center of the chain mail until

the straight wire extends beyond the far end and the hook touches the beginning of the chain mail (wire is shown in red in **photo g**).

**17** Use the hook to capture the first two center rings in the chain mail. Close the hook. Trim the straight wire end ¼" (6mm) past the end of the chain. Use roundnose pliers to make a small hook on this end **(photo h)**. Capture the last two center chain mail rings on this end. Close the hook **(photo i, p. 14)**.

**18** Lightly mark the chain mail piece at the quarter, half, and three-quarters points. Start bending the left quarter chain mail band down. Make the highest point a quarter of the way along. Curve/bend the main (right) part of the band down. Three quarters along, curve the end up to sit even with the initial end. Adjust the length of the piece until the span of the final piece is 3½".

## DESIGN ALTERNATIVE»

Make two shorter vines with closure hooks on both ends, and attach directly to earring wires for easy earrings.

i

j

### CONNECT THE VINES TO THE CHAIN MAIL

**19** Line up the three curved pieces in this order: the vine with the closure loop, the piece of chain mail, and the vine with the closure hook **(photo j)**.

The curves on this bracelet both compress and extend the loops and rings. For the connections to "look right," don't connect them at the halfway points on each piece. Count from the left.

**20** Use a 3mm ring to connect the left edge ring of the chain mail band and the eighth loop of the vine with the closure loop. Repeat on the right edge of the chain mail with the ninth loop of the vine with closure loop.

**21** Connect the end of the vine left hook to the tenth ring on the bottom edge of the chain mail. Connect the right end loop of the vine into the eleventh edge ring on the bottom edge of the chain mail.

**22** Connect the end of the second leaf vine left loop to the eleventh edge ring on the top of the chain mail. Connect the end of the second leaf vine right loop to the twelfth edge ring on the top of the chain mail.

**23** Use 3mm rings to connect the left end ring of the right edge of the chain mail into the eighth loop, and the right chain mail ring into the ninth loop on the vine with the closure hook.

**24** Shape the front and back of the bracelet over a 3" bracelet mandrel or form to give the piece a gentle curve. Form the main side curves at the point where the chain mail connects to the vines. Bend this part of the bracelet around a 1½"-diameter dowel or other frame.

Your wrist is more oval than round, so an oval bracelet will be more comfortable to wear.

# Trillium Flower

As with a trillium flower blooming from the mossy undergrowth in deep woods, a single blossom shines more brightly than an entire bouquet. Link flowers and leaves with delicate helm chain mail. Multiple wire gauges give this necklace both strength and detail.

## MATERIALS

**wire**
- 90" (2.28m) 20-gauge, gold
- 160" (4.07m) 24-gauge, gold
- 100" (2.54m) 30-gauge, gold

**jump rings**
- **140** (½ oz.) 4.7mm 20-gauge, gold
- **124** (½ oz.) 3.2mm 20-gauge, silver

**tools**
- pliers kit
- ⅛" (3mm) dowel and wax (optional)

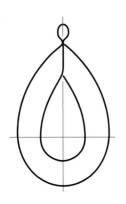

**Figure 1**

a

b

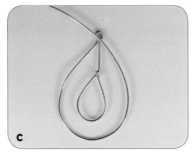

c

### MAKE HELM CHAIN MAIL

**1** Make two 2" (5cm) and two 4" (10cm) pieces of **helm chain mail** using 4.7mm jump rings (large) and 3.2mm jump rings (small) (p. 103).

### MAKE A TRILLIUM PETAL FRAME

**2** Refer to **figure 1** as you create the petals. Cut 8" (20cm) of 20-gauge wire. Make a small, open hook at one end using the tips of your roundnose pliers.

**3** Use your thumb or work carefully with roundnose pliers to make a teardrop shape: Bend the wire out, around, and back up to the hook **(photo a)**. Catch the working wire in the

hook, and close and compress the hook.

**4** Straighten the wire above the teardrop **(photo b)**. Mark a point ⅜" (9mm) along the working wire. At the mark, make an **unwrapped loop**.

**5** At the base of the loop, bend the wire around the teardrop, maintaining ¼" (6mm) spacing between the inside and the outside teardrop loops **(photo c)**.

**6** Use the tail of the working wire to finish wrapping the top loop with three wraps, ending at the back **(photo d)**. Make five trillium petal frames.

### MAKE A VINE

**7** Make a double back-to-back row of **side-by-side coil loops** with 24-gauge wire around a ⅛" (3mm) dowel.

Waxing the dowel before wrapping makes it easier to remove the finished coil.

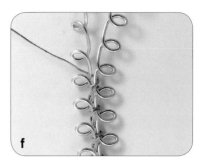

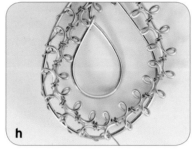

**8** Remove the wire from the dowel. Compress the coil, using your fingers or nylon-jaw pliers to flatten the loops **(photo e)**.

Compressing the coil is easiest if the beginning of each wrap stays in position. If the coil is wrapped from left to right with the wrap in a clockwise direction, press the coil top to the right to retain the loops crossover at the bottom.

**9** Stretch the coil, occasionally compressing the loops back so they lay flat. Continue stretching until the loops are side by side and not overlapping. Stretch the coil a bit more to allow space between the loops.

**10** Bend the stretched coil in half, making sure the loops are facing out.

**11** Using 24-gauge wire, make two wraps at the open end around the base of the paired loops, and position the wire between the next set. Repeat to wrap the entire folded length and make a double vine **(photo f)**.

**ATTACH THE VINE TO THE FRAME**
**12** Lay the double vine across the vertical wire between the two teardrops, with one end extending ³/₁₆" (5mm) beyond the wire. Bend that end around the wire, and compress.

**13** Curve the vine between the two wires **(photo g)**. Trim the second vine end so it lies just behind the first end and is even with the wire frame.

**14** Cut a 20" (51cm) piece of 30-gauge sewing wire. Leave a 1" (2.5cm) wire tail, and stitch the outside of the vine to the frame using an **overcast stitch (photo h)**. Bring the sewing wire over the vertical transition wire, and repeat to stitch the inside of the vine to the center frame. Twist both ends of the sewing wire together, and trim. Tuck the wire along the transition part of the frame.

**MAKE THE CLASP SET**
**15** Make the hook: Cut 10" (25cm) of 20-gauge wire. Using the tips of roundnose pliers, make a small open loop.

**16** Repeat step 3 and 4, but instead of making an unwrapped loop, make a wire extension for the hook: Mark a point ³/₈" (1cm) along the working wire. Use chainnose pliers to make a sharp bend, and fold the wire back toward the base. Compress the wires, making sure they are flat and parallel.

**17** At the base, continue bending the wire around the teardrop, maintaining ¹/₄" spacing. When you reach the top again, use the wire tail to wrap the wire extension three times, ending at the back.

**18** Repeat steps 7-14.

until the spiral is ½" (1.3cm) wide **(photo j)**. Roll the end of the spiral into a loop, and tuck it underneath the spiral top to finish.

## ASSEMBLE THE NECKLACE

**23** Prepare a spiral for the focal by pulling the last ring of the spiral disk down and to the back. Leave just enough room between the main disk and this rim to slide a ring through.

*Assemble the focal flower and the necklace from the back.*

**24** Lay out three finished petal frames with the wrapped loops pointing out and the spiral disk in the center. Arrange the petals so they are just touching.

**25** Connect two adjoining frames and the rim of the spiral disk with a small ring. Repeat until all of the frames are joined to each other and to the spiral rim **(photo k)**.

**26** Connect a piece of chain mail to the focal by opening the final two rings in the helm weave and connecting the wrapped end loop on a petal frame **(photo l)**.

**27** Open two large rings at the other end of the chain mail, and connect them to the frame base of the next petal.

**19** Make a **clasp hook** with the extension **(photo i, p. 17)**.

**20** To make the loop of the clasp, repeat step 15, then step 3. At a point ³⁄₈" along the working wire, use round-nose pliers to make a large ³⁄₁₆" unwrapped loop. Starting at the base of the loop, shape the wire around the teardrop, maintaining ¼" spacing. Use the tail of the wire to finish wrapping the top loop with three wraps, ending at the back. Make and add a vine.

## SPIRAL CENTER

**21** Cut 6" (15cm) of 20-gauge wire. Make a ⅛" closed loop with roundnose pliers. This loop attaches the spiral to both the trillium petals and the necklace helm chain.

**22** To make the horizontal spiral, refer to **figure 2**: Hold the loop vertically with chainnose pliers. Wrap the wire around the pliers' tip. Remove the pliers and continue wrapping

Top

Side

Bottom

**Figure 2**

j

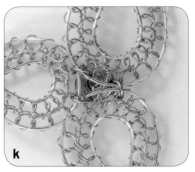

k

l

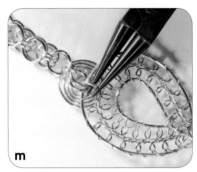

m

**28** Open the loop at the base of a spiral, and connect both the connecting rings and the petal frame. Close the loop **(photo m)**.

**29** Attach the 4" piece of chain mail to the wrapped loop of the petal: Connect both large rings on the end of the chain mail to the wrapped end loop on the petal frame. Open the two large rings at the other end of the chain mail, and connect them to the round base of the clasp petal through the petal frame.

**30** Open the loop at the base of a spiral. Open and slide this loop through to capture both the connecting rings and the petal frame. Close the loop.

**31** Repeat steps 26-30 to complete the other half of the necklace.

## DESIGN ALTERNATIVES»

Double teardrops make beautiful large—but lightweight—earrings.

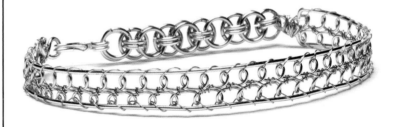

Connect helm chain to a flat, framed vine for a bangle-style bracelet.

# Caged Mail

This simple wire frame is a lovely display case for a focal chain mail flower. The design is simple to execute and very flexible. With the potential of multiple variations, the bail can be made in any shape or size. Shown here as a pendant, it can slide onto chain, a string of beads, or even a scarf.

## MAKE HELM FLOWERS

**1** Make a **helm flower** using 6mm (large) and 4mm (small) jump rings (p. 104).

## BEGIN THE CAGE

**2** Refer to **figure 1** as you create the pendant: Stack the 12" (31cm) twisted and round wires to make a wire set, with the twisted square wire on the bottom. Mark the center point.

The pendant is worked upside down, so the first crossover loop shown at the bottom will eventually be the center top. Complete the crosses with the wires from the left crossing over the top of those coming from the right.

**3** Bend the wire set in half, keeping the wires flat and parallel to each other. Cross the left wire set over the top of the right wire set, leaving a 1/8" (3mm) opening, and continue to bend the wires until they are nearly horizontal.

**4** Bend the wires to cross each other again. This time, leave a 5/16" (8mm) opening (measure or use a dowel) **(photo a)**. Use half-round wire to **bind** and secure these crossover points with two wraps on the bottom and three on the top **(photo b)**.

In the first small loop, the twisted silver wire is on the outside. In the second loop, the gold wire is on the outside. The main body of the pendant will have the twisted silver wire on the outside.

## MATERIALS

**wire**
- 12" (31cm) 20-gauge, round, gold
- 12" 21-gauge, twisted, square, silver
- 12" 21-gauge, half-round, gold

**jump rings**
- **18** 6mm 18-gauge, silver
- **13** 4mm 18-gauge, gold
- **4** 3mm 20-gauge, gold

- 6mm prong-set sew-on rhinestones, garnet red

**tools**
- pliers kit
- 2" (5cm) piece of 1/4" (6mm) dowel (optional)

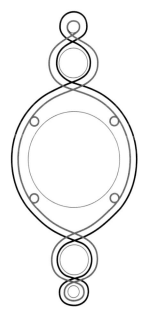

**Figure 1**

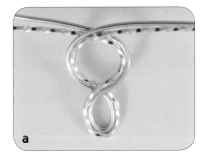

a

b

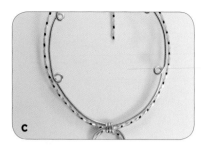

c

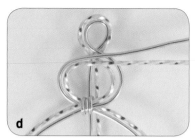

d

e

f

g

**5** Mark the gold (inside) wire 3/4" (1.9cm) from the center of the binding wrap. Make a single-coil loop, facing inward, at this point.

**6** Mark the gold wire 1" (2.5cm) from the single-coil loop. Make a second single-coil loop, facing inward, at this point.

**7** Repeat on the other side from the center **(photo c)**. Bring the twisted wire back into alignment with the looped wire.

**8** Mark each side 3/4" from the second coil loop. Using your fingers or nylon-jaw pliers, bend both sides in an arch so they cross at the mark to create an open oval 1 1/8" wide by 1 1/4" high (2.9x3.2cm). Use half-round wire to bind and secure this crossover; wrap vertically three times.

**9** Bend the wires to cross each other again. This time, leave a 5/16" (8mm) opening (use a dowel, if desired). Make a small single-coil loop with the bottom (right) wire, extending the ends down into the opening. Bring the left crossing wires across the loop base, and wrap once around the base of the coil, ending with the wires to the back **(photo d)**. Secure and trim.

**10** Use half-round wire to secure the crossover by wrapping above the ends of the

pendant wires three times. Fold up the extended wires, going over the ends of the left wrap and the binding wrap. Trim the wires, leaving enough wire to roll the ends toward the pendant. Roll the ends, and compress the entire wire bundle slightly **(photo e)**.

**11** Attach a 4mm ring to the top double loop **(photo f)**.

**ASSEMBLE THE PENDANT**

**12** Center the flower in the frame, with the double helm rings closest to the single-coil frame loops created in step 6. Connect the frame loops to the nearest back large doubled rings in the flower using 3mm rings **(photo g)**.

## DESIGN ALTERNATIVE»

Simplified spirals using a scaled-down version of the shape make beautiful earrings.

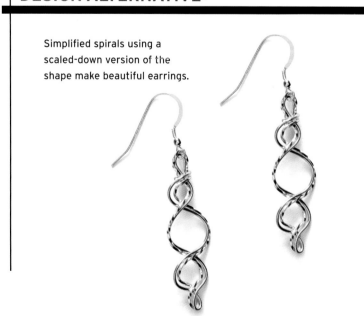

# CHAPTER 2

# Single Wire

# Hydrangea

The petals of this hydrangea paired with narrow strips of chain mail make a huge impact. Wide and bold, this bracelet is still delicate looking and whisper-light to wear.

a

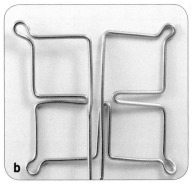

b

## MATERIALS

**wire**
- 50" (1.27m) 20-gauge round, gold

**jump rings**
- **80** 3.2mm 20-gauge, gold
- **23** 3.2mm 20-gauge, silver

**tools**
- pliers kit
- dowel, ³/₈" (1cm) square (optional)
- flush cutters

### MAKE EUROPEAN 4-IN-1 CHAIN MAIL PIECES

**1** Make four 1" (2.5cm) pieces of three-row **European 4-in-1** (p. 101) using 3.2mm jump rings in gold (inner rings) and silver (outer rings).

### MAKE HYDRANGEA FLOWERS

**2** Work with 10" (25cm) of wire and leave a 1" (2.5cm) tail. Using flatnose pliers, make a sharp bend ³/₈" (1cm) from the starting point. ³/₈" from that bend, make an **unwrapped loop** at the corner (horizontal and facing out). ³/₈" from that loop, make a right-angle outside corner, and ³/₈" further, make an inside corner. Repeat once **(photo a)**. Repeat for a third set. For the fourth, repeat but don't make an inside corner. Instead, let the working wire lie over the flower, with the end extending past the center. Make sure that the working wire is on the front. Compress the inside bends slightly with flatnose pliers to help define the flower **(photo b)**.

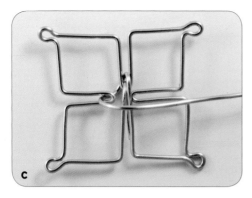

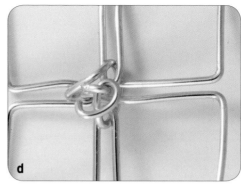

**3** Bring the original tail from the front of the flower across and through the inside opening. Bend the end up. Pull the working wire down and through the same inside bottom bend. Bring the working wire through to the back, then to the front from a side inside bend and make a horizontal wrap **(photo c)**.

**4** Trim the wire tail to ⅛" (3mm). Make a small loop at the end, and place it over the working wire. Close and compress the loop.

**5** Wrap the working wire end around the closed loop, and trim and tuck the wire end **(photo d)**. Repeat steps 2-5 to make a total of four flowers.

### MAKE THE HYDRANGEA HOOK CLASP

**6** Work with 10" of wire again. Make a bend 1" from the end, and mark a point ⅞" (2.2cm) from the bend. Make a sharp bend at this point, bringing the wire end back toward the flower. Compress the wires, making sure that they are straight and flat. This creates an extension for a hook.

The clasp hooks replace the first and second outside corner loops on the first two petals of the hydrangea.

**7** Work ½" (1.3cm) from the end of the wire extension, and continue making a hydrangea flower as in step 2. When you reach the spot for the second corner loop, create a second hook extension instead: Make a sharp bend ½" from the corner, bringing the wire end back toward the flower. Compress the wires and make sure that they are straight and flat **(photo e)**.

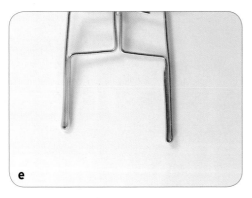

e

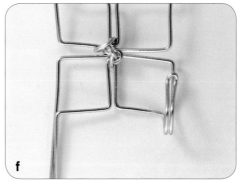

f

**8** Finish making the hydrangea flower as in steps 2-5.

**9** Make a ³⁄₈" **clasp hook** with one wire extension **(photo f)**. Repeat with the other extension.

**ASSEMBLE THE BRACELET**

**10** Connect the chain mail and the flowers with gold rings, linking unwrapped loops to the gold end rings on the chain mail. Connect the hook clasp on one end and a set of rings on the other end for the closure loops.

## DESIGN ALTERNATIVES»

Make smaller shapes and layer for a petite pair of earrings or pendant.

# Triple Twist

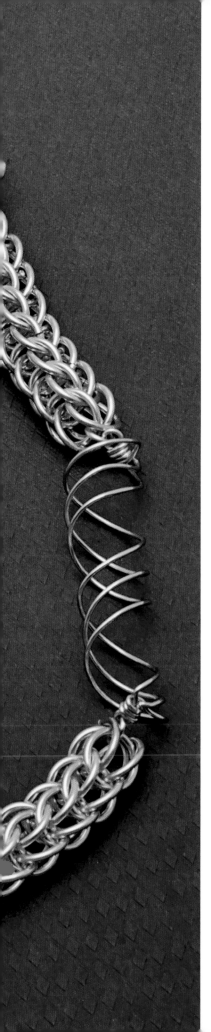

This stylish two-tone rope necklace is made of alternating twisted links of gold wire and silver chain mail. Both strong and lightweight, the necklace uses six twisted wire links connected to segments of chain mail. The pattern has no clasp, creating a fun-to-wear statement piece.

## MAKE FULL PERSIAN CHAIN MAIL SEGMENTS

**1** Make six 2" (5cm) pieces of **full Persian** chain mail (p. 102) using 7.5mm jump rings.

Pre-forming the wire helps to ensure that the wire strands for the twisted link will be spaced evenly and that the wires will stay parallel to each other as the link is formed. The finished bends will appear to be the shoulders, neck, and head of a person.

## MAKE TWISTED WIRE LINKS

**2** Tape or mark one jaw of the roundnose pliers where the diameter is ⅛" (3mm). Use the small end of the pliers' tips to make the first and last bend. (All other curves will use the ⅛" mark.)

## MATERIALS

**wire**
- 90" (2.29m) 20-gauge round, gold

**jump rings**
- **210** (2.5oz) 7.5mm 16-gauge, silver
- **20** 4.5mm 16-gauge, silver

**tools**
- pliers kit
- ³⁄₈" (1cm) dowel, marked or cut at 2" (5cm) long
- twist tie or paper trim
- toothpick

This link design is made using a single piece of wire. Because of the openness of the finished twist, only 15" (38.1cm) of wire is needed to make a 2" (5cm) finished wire link.

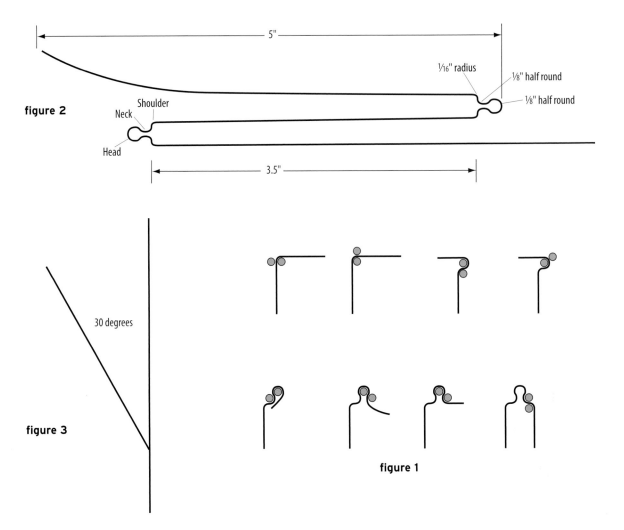

**figure 2**

5"

1/16" radius

1/8" half round

1/8" half round

Shoulder

Neck

Head

3.5"

30 degrees

**figure 3**

**figure 1**

3 Cut a 15" (38cm) piece of wire, and mark it at 5" (13cm). Refer to **figure 1** for the rest of this step: Hold the wire vertically, and place the pliers' tips horizontally at the mark. Bend the wire over the top of one jaw's tips, making a curve with a radius of about 1/16" (2mm). This bend represents the "shoulder."

Turn the pliers vertically and slide them forward to the 1/8" mark so the horizontal part of the wire is between the pliers' jaws.

Pull the wire up and around the top jaw of the pliers back toward the shoulder. This half-circle curve is one side of the "neck."

Make a 1/8" **unwrapped loop** for the "head." Turn the pliers all the way around so the outside jaw is beneath the inside jaw and away from the initial shoulder.

Pull the wire around the bottom pliers' jaw away from the initial shoulder, making a half-circle curve. This half-circle curve forms the other side of the neck.

Remove the pliers, and position the small end of the tip vertically next to the new neck, with the horizontal wire between the pliers' jaws. Pull the wire down over the pliers' tips to form the quarter curve of the second shoulder. Compress the two neck curves until they touch. Do not wrap the base of the loop.

4 Measure 3 1/2" (8.9cm) from the bottom of the last shoulder curve **(figure 2)**. Make the same configuration of shoulder, neck, and head as in step 1. The bends will produce

the new configuration offset and opposite the first one.

5 Straighten out the long wires so they are evenly spaced and parallel **(photo a)**.

6 Place the wire configuration behind a 3/8" (1cm) dowel at a 30-degree angle **(figure 3 and photo b)**.

7 Form the three wires around the dowel, keeping them parallel to each other. Keep the wires in their group of three, spaced apart from the next group of three in the next wrap around the dowel **(photo c)**. This will give a spiral effect. The ends may move and twist, so use chainnose pliers to bring them back into alignment as you curve the piece.

a

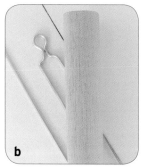

b

c

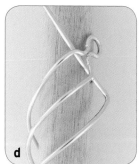

d

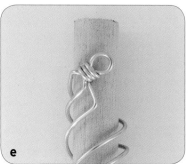

e

f

8 After shaping, use roundnose pliers to make a 90-degree bend in one of the free wire ends. The wire will cross just at the bottom of the compressed neck loop on the inside (dowel side) **(photo d)**.

9 Wrap this working wire around the neck loop three times, ending on the inside. Trim any excess wire, and tuck the end in **(photo e)**.

10 Scoot the entire link up to the edge of the dowel, and place one jaw of the round-nose pliers in the wrapped loop. Carefully bend this loop over the edge until the top of the loop just reaches the center of the spiral opening **(photo f)**. Repeat steps 8–10 on the other end to complete the twisted wire link.

If the link is twisted too tightly around the dowel, use a gentle, unwrapping motion so you can remove the link without permanently altering the shape.

11 Carefully remove the dowel. Adjust the twisted wire link so it measures 2" by gently compressing or stretching the spirals with your hands, if needed.

12 Repeat steps 1–11 for a total of six twisted wire links.

**ASSEMBLE THE NECKLACE**

13 Lay a twisted wire link and a chain mail segment end to end.

14 Spread the top two rings of one chain mail segment apart to expose the rings lying beneath.

15 Connect those exposed rings in the chain mail segment and the end loop of a twisted wire link with a 4.5mm ring.

16 Repeat steps 13–15 to connect the remaining links and chain mail segments. Attach the last segment to the first link.

# Cleo's Charms

Inspired by the Pharaoh's medallions and money, this charm-style bracelet of swirling spirals and squares has a hidden wealth of diamonds in the chain mail weave. These solid square rings stay standing on end with the help of carefully-sized connector rings and the pull of Cleo's charms.

a

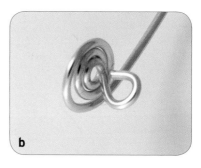

b

## MAKE THE CHAIN MAIL

1 Make 7" (18cm) of **Cleo's helm chain** (p. 104) using 4.8mm (large) and 3.2mm (small) jump rings and 4.8mm square jump rings **(photo a)**.

## MAKE THE CHARMS

2 Cut 12" (31cm) of 20-gauge wire. At the very end of the wire, make a small loop with roundnose pliers.

3 In a plane perpendicular to the loop, begin making a tightly wound spiral that measures $7/16$" (1cm) **(photo b)**.

## MATERIALS

### wire
- 84" (2.13m) 20-gauge round wire, gold
- 56" (1.02m) 24-gauge round wire, gold

### jump rings
- **52** 4.8mm 20-gauge, gold
- **13** 4.8mm closed square, silver
- **50** 3.2mm 20-gauge, silver
- **8** 3mm 20-gauge, gold

- **13** 4mm rose monteé crystals, **6** red and **7** aurora

### tools
- pliers kit

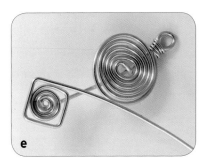

shape, until three more rounds are completed. (Make the diamond the same size as the top spiral.)

**7** End at the point closest to the spiral by wrapping the working wire around the vertical wire. Trim the wire **(photo f)**.

If the diamond does not fit snugly up against the spiral, use roundnose pliers to twist the vertical wire a bit and shorten the charm.

**8** Center a red rose monteé on a 2" (5cm) piece of 24-gauge wire. String both wire ends through the center front of the top spiral. Wrap the ends around the vertical wire behind the spiral, and twist. Trim any excess wire **(photo g)**. Repeat on the diamond spiral with an aurora rose monteé.

**9** Repeat steps 2–8 for a total of six charms.

**MAKE THE CLASP**

**10** Cut 12" (30cm) of 20-gauge wire. At the very end, make a small open loop with the round-nose pliers.

**11** Repeat step 6. The finished diamond will be 7/16" (1.1cm).

**12** Bend the wire up away from the diamond spiral, make a loop on top, and secure

**4** Bend the wire up away from the spiral (but in the same plane), and make an **unwrapped loop** on top.

**5** Catch the small center loop with the wire end. Close the center loop to lock the wire in place **(photo c)**. Secure the top loop with three wraps of 24-gauge wire.

**6** Mark the wire 1/2" (1.3cm) from the bottom of the top spiral. Begin a small spiral in the same plane as the top spiral **(photo d)**, wrapping two full rounds. Begin the diamond shape at the point closest to the top spiral: Make a sharp corner bend with chainnose pliers. Keep the wire in a straight line. One quarter of the way around the center, make another sharp bend. At the bottom, make a sharp bend. At the three-quarter position, make a final sharp bend **(photo e)**.

The bottom piece is now a small center spiral with a diamond frame around it. When the rose monteés are added, the center spiral will not show.

Continue wrapping around the spiral, following the diamond

the loop with three wraps of 24-gauge wire. Catch the small center loop with the wire end.

**13** Extend the working wire beyond the corner of the diamond spiral. Use roundnose pliers to make a U-shaped bend ³⁄₄" (1.9cm) from the diamond point, bringing the working wire back toward the diamond. (This wire extension will be the hook.)

**14** Bring the free end of the hook wire back toward the top loop. Catch the small center loop to lock the position of the wires, and close the loop.

**15** Wrap around the base of the wire extension with the working wire twice.

**16** Hold the piece right side up, and finish making a **clasp hook**.

**17** Add an aurora rose monteé to the clasp as in step 8.

**ASSEMBLE THE BRACELET**
**18** Connect the clasp loop to the two end rings of the chain mail with a 3mm ring.

**19** Connect a charm to every-other square ring in the chain mail: Skip the square ring nearest the clasp, and attach a charm with a 3mm ring. Repeat with the remaining charms.

Attaching the charms will help keep the square rings in the chain mail as diamonds and prevent them from turning and becoming squares.

**20** Make a closure loop for the clasp hook by connecting two 4.8mm gold rings through the final two rings on the opposite end of the bracelet.

## DESIGN ALTERNATIVES »

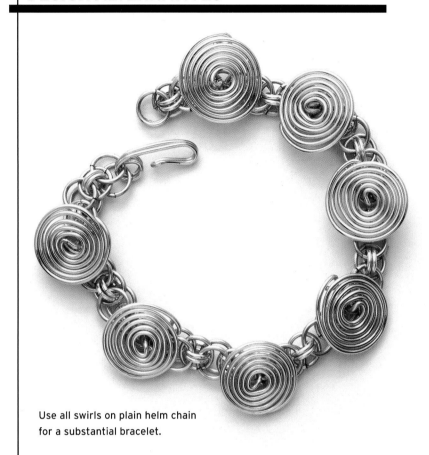

Use all swirls on plain helm chain for a substantial bracelet.

A simple charm makes a great earring.

# Shooting Stars

Who hasn't made a wish on a shooting star? Triple your chances for a wish to come true with this necklace of gold stars and full-Persian two-tone chain mail. Wavy star tails catch and bounce the light, adding extra sparkle. The comfortable chain mail continues around to the back and ends with a beautiful star closure.

## MAKE THE FULL-PERSIAN CHAIN MAIL

**1** Make two 5¼" (13.3cm) and one 3¾" (9.5cm) pieces of **full Persian** chain mail (p. 102) using 7.5mm silver (the first V) and gold (the second V) jump rings.

## MAKE SHOOTING STARS

**2** Cut a 10" (25cm) piece of 20-gauge wire, and make a small hook on one end. Hold the wire horizontally and turn the hook to face away. To make a star, you will make a series of bends ¼" (6mm) apart. Begin ¼" from the hook base and make a sharp upward bend. Measure ¼" and make a downward bend. This is one peak. Repeat once. For the next peak, make the upward bend ¼" from the last bend and make

## MATERIALS

**wire**
- 60" (1.52m) 20-gauge, gold
- 9" (22.9cm) 24-gauge, gold
- 8" (20.3cm) 24-gauge half-round, gold
- 6" (15cm) 16-gauge, gold

**jump rings**
- **125** (1.25oz.) 7.5mm 16-gauge, silver
- **125** 7.5mm 16-gauge, gold
- **3** 6mm 16-gauge, gold

**tools**
- pliers kit
- ½" (1.3cm) dowel
- tape
- tube wringer (optional)

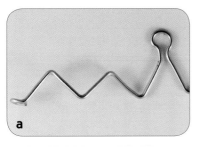

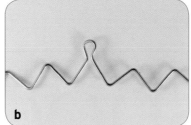

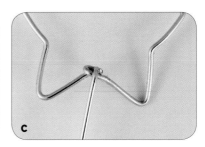

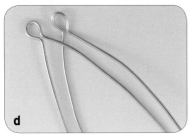

an **unwrapped loop**. Complete the peak with a downward bend **(photo a)**. Make two more peaks for a total of five, with the loop in the center **(photo b)**. Wrap the base of the loop with 24-gauge round wire.

The base of many chainnose pliers' jaws is ¼" (6mm) and can be used as a measuring tool.

3 Use your fingers to bend the peaks around and form a star. Keep the loop at the top.

4 The working tail of the wire will be extra long. Start at the end of the last peak, and bend the wire up across the center front to point toward the top. Using the roundnose pliers' tips, fold the wire back down to form a U shape.

5 Connect the end hook from step 2 to the U shape: The hook needs to catch the back of the U with the long working wire draped down

the front **(photo c)**. Compress the hook to close it. The long wire tail should hang down the middle of the star.

6 Cut two 7" (18cm) pieces of 20-gauge wire to finish the shooting star tail. Make an unwrapped loop at the center of each wire, and bend each wire in half **(photo d)**. Slide a folded wire over the bottom wire of the star on each side of the long wire tail. Compress the base of the loops and center the tail. Flatten the wires, and wrap this bundle with tape ½" (1.3cm) below the loops.

7 Cut a 4" (10cm) piece of 21-gauge half-round wire, and make a square-shaped hook at one end. Wrap the hook around the tail wire bundle, making sure that the open part of the hook is at the back. Compress. Continue wrapping around the bundle six times **(photo e)**, compressing each wrap. Trim the excess wrapping wire, and remove the tape.

8 Begin crimping the tail wires 1" (2.5cm) below the wrap on the tail wires: Use the tip of the chainnose pliers to create waves in each tail wire by bending the wire up and then down

⅛" increments. Stop crimping ½" (1.3cm) before the end of each wire **(photo f)**.

You can also use a tube wringer to crimp all the tails uniformly.

9 Wrap the 16-gauge wire around a ½" dowel, remove the coil from the dowel, and cut three rings. Set one aside to be used later for necklace assembly.

10 Lay the wire ends flat and place a large ring cut in step 9 on top of the bundle. Mark the wires to match the curve of the ring as shown **(photo g)**. (The center wires will be shorter than the outer wires.) Trim the excess wire below these marks.

11 Make a loop at the end of each wire. String each loop on the ring in order **(photo h)**.

12 Repeat steps 2-8, 10, and 11 to make another shooting star.

**MAKE THE STAR CLASP**

13 Repeat steps 2 and 3, but make an extension for the clasp hook instead of an unwrapped loop: Bend the wire

38

g

h

i

j

k

straight up ³/₄" and back down ³/₄" **(photo i)**.

**14** At the end of the last peak, bend the wire up toward the top of the star. Repeat steps 4 and 5 **(photo j)**. At a point ¼" from the connected hooks, make an unwrapped loop. Bring the working wire back up, make a hook, and place the hook over the connection. Trim the tail and close the hook. Wrap the base of the loop with 24-gauge wire six times.

**15** Wrap the base of the top wire extension with 24-gauge wire six times, and make a **clasp hook (photo k)**.

**ASSEMBLE THE NECKLACE**

**16** Lay out the pieces in the following order: the star clasp, a 5¼" piece of chain mail, a shooting star (tail first), the 3³/₄" piece of chain mail, a shooting star, and a 5¼" piece of chain mail.

**17** Begin connecting the components (when attaching the chain mail, go through both inner rings in the weave):

Connect the star clasp hook to the end of a 5¼" piece of chain mail with a 6mm ring.

Connect the top loop of a shooting star to the 5¼" piece of chain mail with a 6mm ring.

Open the large ring at the other end of the shooting star and attach the 3³/₄" piece of chain mail. Close the large ring.

Connect the top loop of a shooting star to the 3³/₄" piece of chain mail with a 6mm ring.

Open the large ring at the other end of the shooting star and attach a 5¼" piece of chain mail. Close the large ring.

Slide the final large ring created in step 9 through the two inside rings on the other end of the 5¼" piece of chain mail.

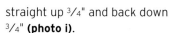

## DESIGN ALTERNATIVE»

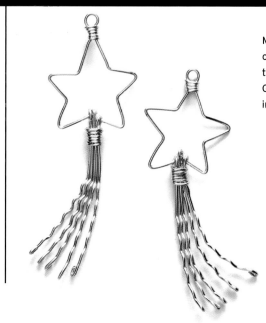

Make stars, add crimped wires, bind together, and voilà! Gorgeous charms in a flash!

# CHAPTER 3

# Multiple Wires

# Draping with Daisies

The delicate, gold draping in this scalloped necklace is accented with two-tone helm flowers and a single garnet crystal. Using multiple fine wires provides the solid look of draped fabric. A simple 2-in-1 chain at the back means this sweet floral necklace can be adjusted easily for length.

## MATERIALS

**wire**
- 16" (38cm) 18-gauge round, gold
- 135" (3.4m) 22-gauge round, gold

**jump rings**
- **45** 4.8mm 20-gauge, gold
- **30** 3.2mm 20-gauge, silver
- **30** 3.2mm 20-gauge, gold

- 4mm bicone crystal, garnet
- 2" (5cm) headpin, gold
- masking tape (optional)

**tools**
- pliers kit
- 16" diameter neckform (optional)

a

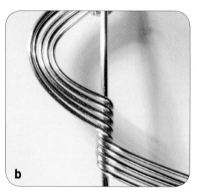
b

### MAKE THE HELM FLOWERS

1 Make three **helm flowers** (p. 104) using five sets of double and five sets of single 4.8mm gold jump rings (large) and five sets of 3.2mm silver jump rings (small) per flower.

### EMBELLISH THE CENTER DAISY BLOOM

2 String a 4mm bicone crystal on a 2" (5cm) headpin. Make a small loop above the crystal, and attach the loop to a large doubled ring in one of the helm flowers. Close the loop.

### MAKE 2-IN-1 CHAIN MAIL CONNECTOR CHAINS

3 Pick up two closed small gold rings with one open small silver ring, and close the ring. Pick up two closed small gold rings and two closed rings on the end of the chain with an open small silver ring. Close the ring. Continue until you have a chain 1¼" (3.2cm) long. Repeat to make a second connector chain.

### MAKE THE DRAPED LINKS

4 Cut a 3½" (8.9cm) piece of 18-gauge wire (this is the base wire). Use the roundnose pliers to make a small loop on each end.

5 Cut five 8" (20cm) pieces of 22-gauge wire (these are the draping wires). Using the roundnose pliers' tips, make a small loop on one end of a wire. Open the loop, hook it over the the base wire, and close the loop. Repeat with each wrapping wire. Position the piece so the base wire is vertical and the draping wires extend to the left just below the top loop. Align the five draping wires and tape, if desired.

6 Hold both the base wire loop and the draping wire closed loops with one hand. Carefully bend the draping wires (as a group) up and around the end of your thumb, keeping the wires flat and parallel **(photo a)**.

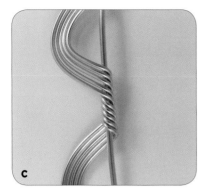

c

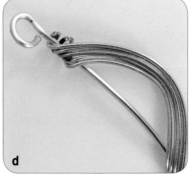

d

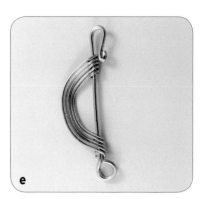

e

7 Bring the draping wires over the front of the base wire, and wrap them all the way around the base wire **(photo b)**. Make an additional half wrap, finishing so the five draping wires are behind the base wire.

8 Place your thumb on the base wire above the wraps. As in step 3, bend the draping wires around your thumb. Bring the draping wires behind the base wire, and wrap them all the way around the base wire. Make an additional half wrap, so the draping wires are in front of the base wire.

9 As in step 6, place your thumb on the base wire above the wraps and bend the draping wires around your thumb **(photo c)**. Mark the draping wires $^3/_{16}$" (5mm) beyond where they cross the base wire. Trim the draping wires on a line parallel to the base wire. Using the round-nose pliers' tips, make a small loop on each wire end. Hook each loop over the base wire **(photo d)**, and close the loops.

10 Using your hands or a neckform, gently bend the entire draped link into a gentle arch, keeping the wire drapes flat and to the outside of the bend.

**MAKE THE DRAPED CLASP**

11 Cut a 3" (7.6cm) piece of 18-gauge wire (this is the base wire). Using the roundnose pliers, make a loop on one end. Close the loop.

12 Cut five 3" pieces of 22-gauge wire (these are the draping wires). As in step 5, make a small loop on one end of each wire, hook the open loops over the base wire, and close the loops. Position the piece so the base wire is vertical and the draping wires extend to the right just below the top loop. Align the five draping wires and tape, if desired.

13 Bend the draping wires around your thumb and connect them to the base wire as in step 9.

14 Use the roundnose pliers' tips to make a small loop on the other end of the base wire. Place one jaw inside the loop. Place the other jaw on top of the base wire $^1/_4$" (6mm) from the loop. Bend the loop end up and over to make a hook **(photo e)**.

## ASSEMBLE THE NECKLACE

**15** Start in the center front: Connect an end loop of a draped unit and a single large gold ring in the outside rim of the center daisy bloom (the ring that spans the double silver rings of the flower) with a large gold ring **(photo f)**.

**16** Use a large gold ring to connect the end loop of the draped link and a large gold ring in the side flower **(photo g)**.

Pay attention to the curve of the draped links as you connect each piece so the final necklace hangs correctly.

**17** Skip a single large gold ring position on the helm flower. Connect the next available single large gold ring to a draped link with a large gold ring.

**18** Connect a connector chain to the last loop of the end draped link with a large gold ring.

**19** Repeat steps 15–18 to assemble the other side of the necklace.

**20** Connect the clasp to the necklace: On one end of the necklace, attach the loop of the clasp element to the final ring (or rings) in the connector chain. Connect a large gold ring to the final rings on the other end of the necklace **(photo h)**.

## DESIGN ALTERNATIVE»

Use shorter base and wrapping wires to make easy earring links. Experiment with gauges and metals to get the look you desire.

# Rose and Thorns

This handsome bracelet carries the romance of a single rose captured in brambles. The design is not as complex as it may first appear; take each step one at a time. If you want something to wear quickly, the individual pieces can stand alone as a pendant or a band.

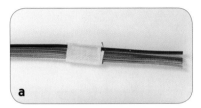

a

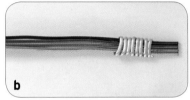

b

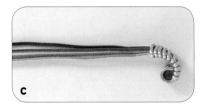

c

## MATERIALS

### wire
- 15" (38cm) 20-gauge round in each of **3** colors: light pink, medium pink, dark pink
- 19" (48cm) 20-gauge round, dark purple
- 18" (45.7cm) 20-gauge round, gold
- 10" (25cm) 21-gauge half-round, gold
- 71" (1.80m) 22-gauge round, gold

### jump rings
- **150** (1 oz.) 6mm 18-gauge, silver
- **130** (.5 oz.) 4mm 18-gauge, gold

- masking tape

### tools
- pliers kit
- bracelet mandrel (optional)

## MAKE THE HELM CHAIN

1 Make a 14½" (36.8cm) piece of **helm chain** (p. 103) using 18-gauge 6mm silver jump rings (large) and 18-gauge 4mm gold jump rings (small). Connect the two ends of the chain with two large rings (following the pattern of the weave).

## MAKE THE ROSE

While this rose looks freeform, it has a structure. The wire is first wound into a spiral, then bent into a triangle, then bent into a square spiral. Four petals in the form of half-circles are added at each corner of the square. Finally, the remaining wire captures everything in a circle.

2 Line up 15" (38cm) of 20-gauge wire in the following order: dark purple, dark pink, medium pink, and light pink. Tape around the wires at the working end to keep them flat and parallel **(photo a)**.

You can make a lot of the twists and turns by hand. If you want to use tools on some of the larger bends, choose nylon-

jaw pliers so the wire colors don't chip.

3 Use 21-gauge half-round wire to **bind** the group of wires with at least eight wraps, leaving a ½" (1.3cm) tail. Trim the wire ends to ¼" (6mm) beyond the wraps so the wire ends are even **(photo b)**.

4 Use roundnose pliers to roll up the short wire ends **(photo c)**. Continue rolling to include the eight binding wraps and colored wires until you have formed a coil for the rose center. The binding wraps will separate slightly. Remove the tape.

If you have not worked with multiple wires before, practice with a single wire first. These practice pieces have a charm of their own and can easily be turned into earrings to match your bracelet.

5 Refer to **figure 1** as you form the rose: Use your fingers to spread the wires slightly. Pull the individual colors one at a time to encircle the flower center, placing

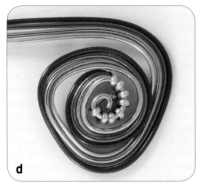

d

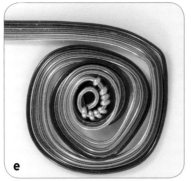

e

f

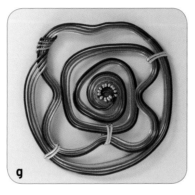

g

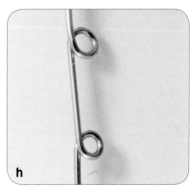

h

Spiral          Spiral triangle          Spiral square

Corner petals                    Circle and end tuck

**Figure 1**

them next to each other so that the bundle of wires is flat and tight in a horizontal plane around the center coil.

**6** Make a complete spiral circle in the flower center.

**7** Make a spiral triangle around the circle. The corners will be slightly rounded **(photo d)**.

**8** Make an encircling spiral square around the triangle **(photo e)**. Use half-round wire to bind the final side of this newly formed square to the previous triangle spiral with two wraps **(photo f)**.

**9** Create a series of rose petals: Make a petal by first extending the wires directly away from the square. Hold the wires firmly with the thumb and index finger of your non-wrapping hand (or nylon-jaw pliers). Pull the end of the working wires back toward the center on the side of the previous square. Pull the end toward the center and beyond the edge. Hold the wire in place at the edge with the thumb and index finger of your non-wrapping hand. Pull the end of the working wires away from the center of the rose. Back the petal indent up to just touch the flat edge of the square. Repeat this step three times.

It is not necessary to bind the base of each petal to the square spiral below; add only enough binding wraps to keep the rose from flexing too much.

**10** Pull the working wire around to encircle the entire row of petals. Bind the circle wires to the top of a petal or two with two wraps of half-round wire.

**11** With the entire rose encircled, trim the excess colored wire, leaving a 2" (5cm) tail. Using flatnose pliers, make a right-angle bend in the wires where they cross. Loop the wire ends over the front of the closest petal. Wrap the wires around the petals a second time, bringing the wire ends to the back. Compress the wraps tightly, and trim the excess wire **(photo g)**.

**THORNY BRAMBLE**

**12** Cut 48" (1.22m) of 22-gauge wire. Using the roundnose pliers' tips, make a very small loop every ³⁄₈" (1cm) along the wire. Make sure the loops face the same direction **(photo h)**.

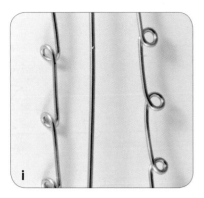

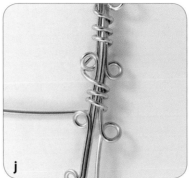

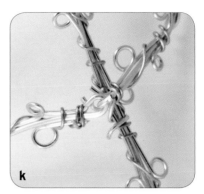

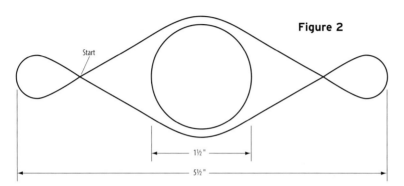

**Figure 2**

Start

1½"

5½"

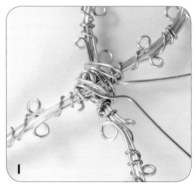

**13** Use flatnose pliers to flatten the loops. Fold the looped wire in half with the loops facing out.

**14** Cut an 18" (46cm) piece of 20-gauge gold wire, and place it between the two rows of looped wires **(photo i)**. Hold the wires flat and tightly together. Tape the wires to keep the wires flat and parallel.

**15** Wrap 22-gauge wire around the wire bundle near the end several times.

**16** Continue to the next space between a set of loops. Wrap two or three times, and then continue to the space between the next set of loops. Repeat **(photo j)** until the entire wire bundle is wrapped.

**17** Bend the wire bundle into the configuration shown, starting and stopping at the point where the wires cross **(figure 2)**.

Make a small loop in the center 20-gauge wire at each end of the bramble. Connect the loops together, and compress them to make sure they're tightly connected **(photo k)**. Trim any excess wrapping wire.

**18** Use 22-gauge wire to make untidy wraps at the points where the bramble wires cross **(photo l)**.

**MAKE THE HOOK**

**19** Cut a 2" (5cm) piece of 20-gauge gold wire, and make a **clasp hook**. Use roundnose pliers to roll the wire ends opposite the hook into loops (for connecting).

**ASSEMBLE THE BRACELET**

**20** Lay out the circle of helm chain. Flatten and stretch the circle horizontally so you have two "ends." Connect two small rings to each end (two large rings in the helm chain weave). Connect

two large rings to each pair of small rings you just added.

**21** Lay out the helm chain circle again (with the added rings to the right and left), and place the thorny bramble in the center. Adjust the chain mail to match the bramble center and touch the top and bottom of the bramble end loops.

**22** Where there is contact with the helm chain, use chainnose pliers to adjust the bramble loops to sit at right angles to the thorny bramble loops **(photo m)**. Connect the thorny bramble and the chain mail with rings in the helm chain.

**23** Cut 4" (10.2cm) of dark purple wire and wrap it around a jaw of the roundnose pliers (at about the midpoint) three or four times. Remove the coil, and cut three or four rings. Place the rose in the center of the bramble, and use the dark purple

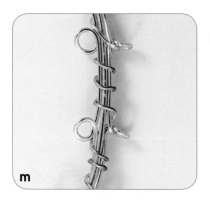

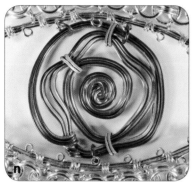

rings to attach it to the thorny
bramble through the nearest
bramble loop **(photo n)**.

24 Connect the loops on the
clasp hook to the two
large rings on one side of the
bracelet. (The two end rings on
the other end of the bracelet will
catch the hook.)

25 Bend the front and back
of the bracelet over a
mandrel or other form to give a
gentle curve: Form the main
side curves at the points where
the chain mail connects to the
bramble. Bend this part of the
bracelet around a dowel or other
frame of about 1½" (3.8cm) in
diameter to create an oval shape.

Single-wire practice
shapes make cute
earrings and pendants.

# Stars of the Sea

A double row of chain mail scallop shells supports an extraordinary starfish—with two dainty baby starfish alongside and a bonus starfish clasp. This eye-catching necklace is sure to turn heads!

## MATERIALS

**wire**
- 30" (76.2cm) 20-gauge, gold
- 280" (7.11m) 24-gauge, gold
- 216" (5.48m) 24-gauge, silver

**jump rings**
- **40** 7mm 16-gauge, gold
- **782** (3.25 oz.) 3.25mm 18-gauge, silver
- **4** 4mm 18-gauge, silver

**tools**
- pliers kit
- 1/8" (3mm) dowel
- tape

a

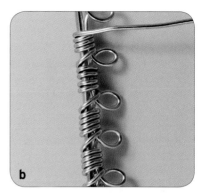

b

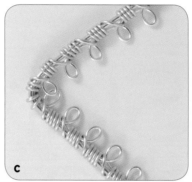

c

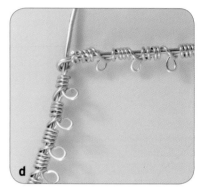

d

### MAKE SCALLOP CHAIN MAIL

**1** Make 18" (46cm) of **scallop chain mail** (p. 105) using 7mm 16-gauge (large) and 3.25mm 18-gauge (small) jump rings. (You will need 39 base chains.)

### MAKE A CENTER STAR

**2** Use 24-gauge silver wire to make 12" (31cm) of 1/8" (3mm) spaced **side-by-side loops (photo a)**.

**3** Stack the side-by-side loops with 12" (30cm) of 20-gauge gold wire, and use 24-gauge gold wire to **bind** the two wires together (wrap four times around the ends). Using the same length of wire, continue to the next loop opening, and wrap four times. Repeat **(photo b)** until you have 11 3/4" (29.8cm) of wrapped loops.

**4** Unwrap 1/4" (6mm) of the wrapping wire, and trim 1/4" of the side-by-side loop wires. Use roundnose pliers to make a small hook on the end of the 20-gauge wire so only the hook shows.

**5** Mark ten 3/4" (1.9cm) increments on the bundled wires, starting at the top of the loop. At the first 3/4" mark, bend the wire sharply down to create a peak. 3/4" farther along, bend the wire sharply up, and 3/4" farther along, bend the wire sharply down **(photo c)**. Repeat three more times for a total of five peaks.

**6** Trim the bundled wire 1/4" beyond the base of the last peak. Unwrap 1/4" of wrapping wire, and trim the side-by-side loops wires 1/4" **(photo d)**. Make a hook on the end of the 20-gauge wire. Use your finger to bend the peaks around and make a star shape, and connect the two end hooks. Close the hooks.

### MAKE THREE SMALL STARS

**7** Use 24-gauge silver wire to wrap 4 1/2" (11.4cm) of

20-gauge wire to make a tight **coil (photo e)**.

**8** Unwrap 1/4" worth of wrapping wire. Use round-nose pliers to make a small hook on the end of the 20-gauge wire. Hold the wire horizontally and turn the hook to face away. 3/8" (1cm) from the finished hook base, bend the wire sharply down to make a peak, and 3/8" further, make another bend up **(photo f)**. Repeat four times for a total of five peaks.

**9** Repeat step 6, omitting the side-by-side loop wire **(photo g)**.

**10** Cut a 15" (38cm) piece of 24-gauge gold wire to complete the decorative center wrap. Fold the wire in half. (You will be wrapping with two wires, even though the photo shows one wire for clarity.) Leave a 1/4" tail over the closed hooks. Bring the working wire up across the star and to the left of the

e

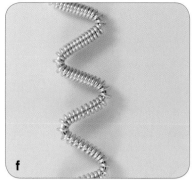

f

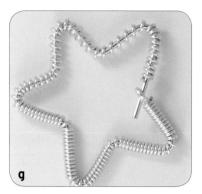

g

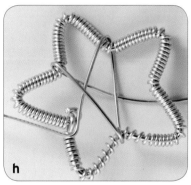

h

i

j

opposite center peak. Wrap in front of the star, and bring the wires behind, continuing over to the next counter-clockwise opening. Bring the wires across the star and to the left space of the previously wrapped peak, moving counter-clockwise from the first wrap. Continue **(photo h)** until each center dent has a double wire wrap. The back of the star will have the same pattern.

**11** Make a hook in the original tail of wrapping wire and in the end of the wrapping wire where it crosses. Connect the hooks. Use pliers to coax the hooks to the back. Repeat steps 7-11 for a total of three small stars.

### MAKE A STAR CLASP

**12** Repeat step 7. Unwrap 3/4" of wrapping wire. Use roundnose pliers to make a small hook on the end of the center 20-gauge wire. Hold the wire

horizontally and turn the hook to face away. At a point 3/8" from the finished hook base, bend the wire sharply down to make a peak, and 3/8" further, make another bend up. Repeat four times for a total of five peaks. Trim the working wire 2" beyond the last peak.

Both the starting wire tail and the working wire extend beyond the peak **(photo i)**.

**13** Mark a point 3/4" beyond the peak on the working wire. Use roundnose pliers to make a sharp U bend for a wire extension. Compress the extension.

**14** Use the initial tail wire to wrap the base of the U bend five times **(photo j)**.

**15** Repeat steps 10 and 11.

**16** Make a hook in the original tail of wrapping wire and in the end of the working wire where it crosses. Connect the hooks, trim the wire, and use pliers to coax the hooks to the back.

k

**17** Set the piece right side up, and use the wire extension to finish making a **clasp hook**.

**ASSEMBLE THE NECKLACE**

**18** Connect the star clasp to the chain mail with two 3.25mm rings **(photo k)**.

**19** Complete the center star by placing a small star in its middle. The points of the small star should just touch the deepest indents of the center star. Connect these two pieces with 3.25mm rings through each small star peak and around each center star indent.

**20** Attach the center star to the chain mail by turning one of the small loops at a right angle to the center star and sliding the large center ring from the chain through this loop.

**21** The small side stars are connected with two peaks hugging a scallop: Connect a large ring in the chain mail and the peak of a side star with a 4mm 18-gauge ring. Match the second side star peak up with the next large outside ring. Connect the large ring in the chain mail and the second peak of the side star with a 4mm ring. Repeat on the opposite side.

## DESIGN ALTERNATIVES»

Insert a brilliant crystal chaton or rose montee in the center of a star for a colorful twist on the design.

A plain star in rustic copper results in an airy pendant.

# Valley Ferns

Both the front and back of this necklace use sections of diagonal Byzantine to provide the focal impact of deep V shapes. Open wirework frames of gold and twisted silver lighten the piece while framing the curling, graduated ferns. The closure is in the front, masquerading as simple framing, and hiding in plain sight.

## MATERIALS

**wire**
- 100" (2.54m) 20-gauge, gold
- 40" (1.02m) 20-gauge, silver
- 50" (1.27m) 21-gauge twisted square, silver
- 20" (51cm) 21-gauge half-round, silver
- 30" (76m) 24-gauge, silver-colored non-tarnish copper

**jump rings**
- **340** (2oz) 4mm 18-gauge, silver
- **50** 6mm 18-gauge, gold
- **2** 8mm 18-gauge, gold
- **16** 4.8mm square, gold

**tools**
- pliers kit
- pencil or sharpened dowel
- permanent marker

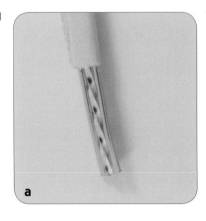

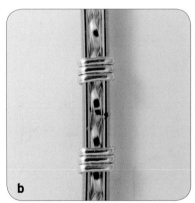

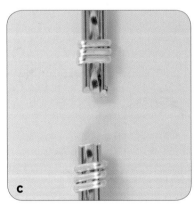

### MAKE DIAGONAL BYZANTINE CHAIN MAIL

1 Make two **diagonal Byzantine** (p. 98) V-shaped pieces using 4mm jump rings (small), 6mm jump rings (medium), and 8mm jump rings (large). Make 11 diagonal Byzantine segments for one V and make 15 diagonal Byzantine segments for the other.

### MAKE THE FRAMES

2 Make the compound wire for the frame: Cut two 11" (28cm) pieces of 20-gauge round gold wire and one 11" piece of 21-gauge twisted silver. Lay the pieces out in a tight, flat bundle in this order: one round wire, one twisted square wire, and one round wire. Tape the ends **(photo a)**.

3 Mark the bundle 4" (10cm) from one end, leave a ¼" (6mm) space, mark 3" (8cm) farther, leave a ¼" space, mark

1½" (4cm) farther, leave a ¼" space, and mark 1" (2.5cm) farther. **Bind** the bundle with three wraps of half-round silver wire on each side of the ¼" spaces **(photo b)**. Flush-cut the wires between the wraps **(photo c)**. Repeat steps 1 and 2 to make a total of four sets of cut compound wires.

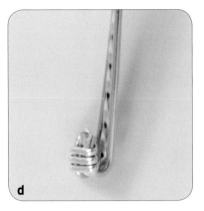

d

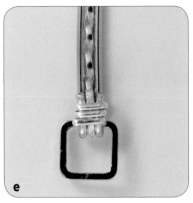

e

f

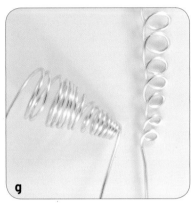

g

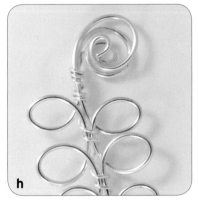

h

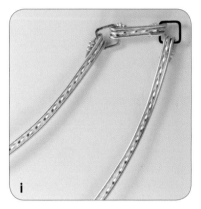

i

4 Use roundnose pliers to make a small hinge on each end of each compound wire by rolling the free ends in **(photo d)**.

*Grasp the wires carefully so the binding wraps don't slide off. The binding wires will keep the wires on the front from spreading without an extra wrap.*

String a closed square ring on the hinge at the end of each 3" and 4" compound wire. Close the hinge **(photo e)**. Compress the wire on the connections where less movement is desired **(photo f)**.

5 Lay out the compound wires: Place a 4" compound wire to sit vertically. Place a 3" compound wire to the right (to the inside). Connect each end of these compound wires to a closed square ring.

6 Connect a 1½" (3.8cm) compound wire to the two square rings at the bottom of the layout, and connect a 1" compound wire to the two square rings at the top. Repeat steps 4-6 to make three more frames.

**MAKE TWO GRADUATED FERNS**

7 Create **graduated loops**: Fold a 20" (51cm) piece of wire in half. Starting 1" from the folded end and using just one of the wires, make a coil cone. Start at the small end of the cone, and wrap around a cone-shaped dowel to make 12 wraps. Repeat with the other wire. Flatten and expand the cones **(photo g)**.

8 Line up both of the wires so the bottoms touch and are parallel. Adjust the coil loops so they are directly across from each other.

9 Use 24-gauge wire to make six wraps around the base wires at the large loop end. Then, moving up one set of loops at a time, wrap twice between each loop set. At the last (smallest) loop, make five wraps.

10 Use roundnose pliers to spiral the wires on the small end. Make a slightly larger spiral on the large loop end **(photo h)**. Repeat steps 7-10 to make another graduated fern.

**MAKE THE CLASP**

11 The clasp is a variation of connecting extension pieces of 1½" and a 2" (5cm) compound wire. Make a connector hook at one end **(photo i)**.

12 On the other end, and on the front of the piece below the binding wires, roll the ends

Stack three wires, curve around dowels, and bind as desired for a lovely freeform pendant.

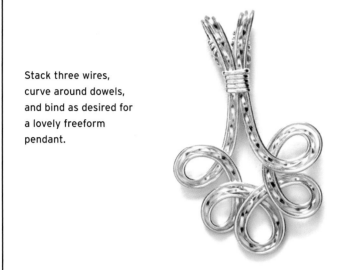

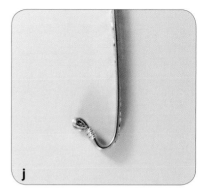

Make curvy loops for an elegant and easy pair of earrings.

of the wires back and tuck them against the binding wires. Flip the bundle to the back, and bend the tip up and over a chainnose pliers' jaw to make a clasp hook **(photo j)**.

13 Attach the hinge end of the 1½" piece to the square ring on the inside bottom of the top frame. Close the hinge. Attach the connector end of the 2" clasp hinge end to the square ring on the outside bottom of the top frame. Close the hinge ring. The clasp hooks can catch the square rings immediately below them to close the clasp.

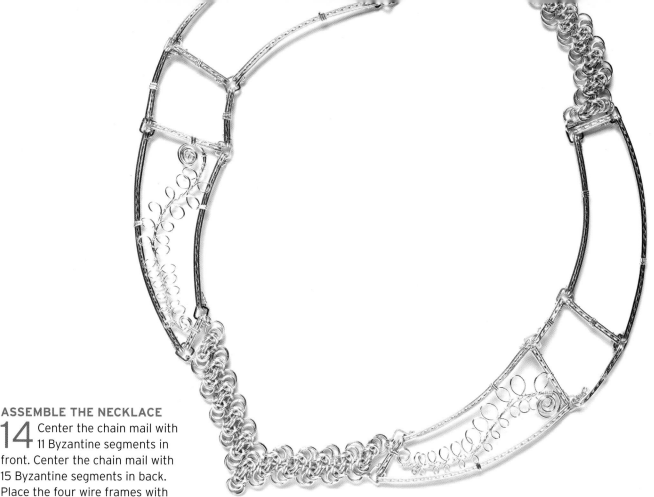

## ASSEMBLE THE NECKLACE

**14** Center the chain mail with 11 Byzantine segments in front. Center the chain mail with 15 Byzantine segments in back. Place the four wire frames with the smaller end of the frame at the very bottom and top, as these will connect with the chain mail. Space the wide frame ends about 1" (2.5cm) apart (leaving room for the extenders on one side of the necklace and the double clasp on the other).

**15** Attach the top of the front chain mail to a fern frame: Connect a 4mm ring, a 6mm ring, and the square ring at the bottom of the frame. Repeat for the other side of the frame.

**16** Attach the top of the back chain mail to an open frame (no fern) by connecting a 4mm ring to the last 6mm ring and the square ring at the top of the frame. Repeat on the other side of the frame.

**17** Add two extension pieces to one side of the frame: Prepare a 1½" (3.8cm) piece with hooked ends, and string through the bottom outside square ring on the top piece and the top outside square ring on the bottom piece. Close the hooks. Prepare a 1" piece with hooked ends, and string through the bottom inside square ring on the top piece and the top inside square ring on the bottom piece. Close the hooks **(photo k)**.

**18** Assemble the fern in the frame: Orient the fern piece so the larger spiral and larger end of the fern are at the wider end of the frame. Bind the fern in place at the top, bottom,

and each side with two wraps of half-round wire, sliding it through the loops of the fern closest to the wire frame and around the frame. Compress these wires. Repeat on the other side of the necklace. Take care to make the bindings on each side of the necklace as symmetrical as possible.

To make this necklace even more comfortable to wear, gently curve the frames to make a rounder "V." The frames high on the shoulders can also be arched: Gently bend the assembled frames over a form so the pieces will follow the contour of your neckline.

# CHAPTER 4

# Frames

# Diamond Solitaire

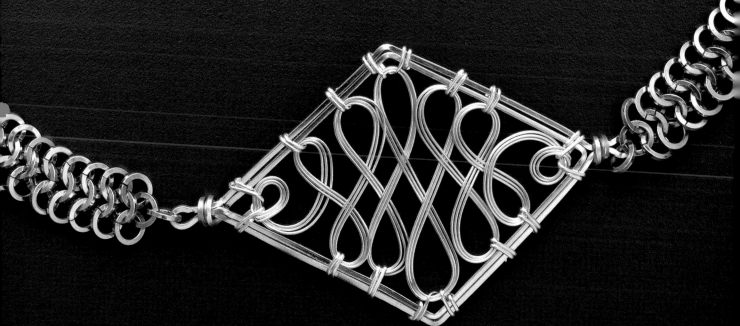

Timeless and beautiful, this necklace is composed of a pair of standout diamonds with center scroll detail. The choker is elegant, refined, and best of all: shiny! Paired with European 4-in-1 in fashionable square wire, these diamonds don't need to wait for a black tie event.

## MATERIALS

**wire**
- 28" (71.1cm) 20-gauge square, silver
- 105" (2.67m) 24-gauge round, silver

**jump rings**
- **290** (3 oz.) 5mm 18-gauge square wire, sterling silver

**tools**
- pliers kit

**Figure 1**

### MAKE EUROPEAN 4-IN-1 PIECES

1 Make two 6¼" (15.9cm) pieces of **European 4-in-1** (p. 101) using 5mm jump rings.

### MAKE THE FOCAL DIAMOND

2 Refer to **figure 1** as you complete the focal diamond. First, make the frame: Cut a 16" (40cm) piece of 20-gauge square wire.

3 Use flatnose pliers to bend the wire 30 degrees 1" (2.5cm) from the end. Mark four 1½" (3.8cm) sections along the wire. Make three more consecutive bends at these marks: Bend the wire 120 degrees, 60 degrees, and 120 degrees to make a diamond shape. Use tape to bind the bands together while making the second row. Keep the square wire flat and snug to the first row on all sides.

The second wire frame sits right outside of the first frame. The starting tail is below the second layer of bends. The corners on the second frame will have a more gentle bend at each corner to accommodate the outside radius of the first frame.

4 At the first corner, bend the wire away from the frame. Use roundnose pliers to make an **unwrapped loop**. Make the base of the loop tight and close to the corner of the band below, but do not add wraps at this time **(photo a)**.

5 Using flatnose pliers, bend the wire to follow the second side of the diamond. Make a second bend at the top of the frame so the wire is lined up to follow the third side of the diamond.

6 At the third corner, make a second unwrapped loop by bending the wire away from the frame. Use roundnose pliers to shape the loop **(photo b)**.

7 Using flatnose pliers, bend the wire to follow the fourth side of the frame. The wire end will be near the beginning wire tail and should be placed below the unwrapped loop but above the original tail.

8 End the frame by wrapping the first loop twice with the original tail wire: This wire is in position below the loop. Capture the extension of the working wire. Bring the initial tail wrapping wire up, and go across the top of the loop **(photo c)**. Make a second wrap **(photo d)**, ending at the back. Trim the ends. Bend the extension of the working wire down over the top of the double wrap. Trim this wire, and roll the end toward the frame. Compress the entire wrap slightly.

**9** Use a new wire to wrap the loop from step 6 twice, keeping both ends at the back **(photo e)**.

**MAKE THE SCROLL CENTER**
**10** Cut three 20" (51cm) pieces of 24-gauge wire. Leave a ½" (1.3cm) tail with all three wires, and make a ¼" (6mm) loop with the bundle. Fold the tail end over the working end, and compress. Trim any wire ends that hang beyond the loop wires **(photo f)**. Be sure all the wires sit flat and side by side. (Use your fingers or nylon-jaw pliers.)

*As you make the turns, the individual wires will move relative to each other.*

**11** Make gentle curves and loops while creating figure 8s in increasing and then decreasing sizes (five total). Always cross the working wire over the top **(photo g)**. When you reach the end, make a final loop with the bundle **(photo h)**. Fold each wire end, wrap them over the loop, and tuck them to the back. Trim any extensions that show beyond the wires, and compress this end of the scroll center.

**12** Use 21-gauge half-round binding wire to secure the scroll center to the frame. Place the scroll center in the frame, and start with the top center loop: **Bind** with one wrap over the frame only to one side of the top peak.
On the second wrap, include the top center loop of the scroll center. Allow sufficient room for the figure bundle to remain flat.
Make a third wrap by bringing the half-round wire through the loop and wrapping both the scroll

 a
 b
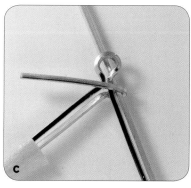 c
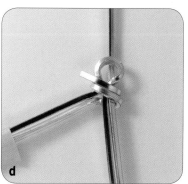 d
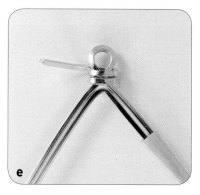 e
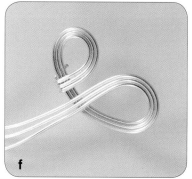 f
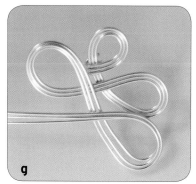 g
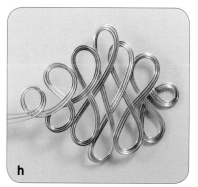 h

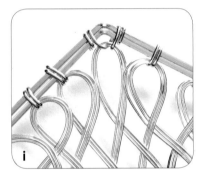

and around the frame. Continue by bringing the wire through the loop and wrapping both the figure and the scroll frame above the loop once. Make the final wrap over the frame only, trim, and compress the wrapping wires. Repeat to secure the other loop end to the other side of the frame.

**14** Bind each remaining scroll center loop to the frame with two wraps of half-round wire. Compress the wraps **(photo i)**.

**MAKE THE SMALL CLASP DIAMOND**

**15** Refer to **figure 2** as you complete the small clasp diamond, using 12" (30cm) of 20-gauge wire. Repeat step 2 and 3, except mark four 1" sections along the wire to begin.

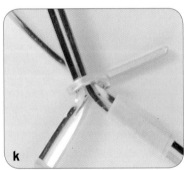

**16** At the first corner, bend the wire away from the frame. Use roundnose pliers to make a wire extension by measuring ³⁄₄" (1.9cm) out from the work. At this mark, make a sharp U bend and bring the wire back to the frame. Compress the extension, but do not finish wrapping at this time **(photo j)**.

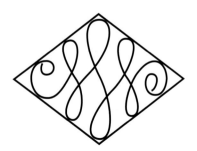

center and the frame on the other side of the corner once.

Make the fourth (and final) wrap over the frame only. Compress these wraps. Secure the bottom center loop to the other side of the frame in the same way. Compress the wrapping wires.

**13** Use half-round wire to secure the loop ends of the center scroll to the frame. Make one wrap over just the frame below the loop. On the second wrap, include the scroll center wire by going through the loop

**Figure 2**

**m**

**17** Continue following steps 5-8 **(photo k)**.

**18** Turn the frame to view the front. Using roundnose pliers, finish making a **clasp hook** with the wire extension **(photo l)**.

**19** Use short pieces of square wire to finish wrapping the unwrapped loop on the other end, keeping the wire ends at the back.

Complete the scroll center for the clasp as with the focal diamond, but make fewer loops to fit into the smaller frame.

**20** Repeat steps 10-14. Use half-round wire to bind the scroll center to the frame. Complete the center first, and then move to the ends. Finally, work the remaining loops. Trim and compress all of the wires.

**ASSEMBLE THE NECKLACE**

**21** Attach the chain mail to the center front focal diamond with a square ring. Repeat on the other side of the diamond.

**22** On one end of the necklace, connect the loop of the diamond clasp with a square ring.

**23** On the other end of the necklace, connect a final square ring that will act as the catch for the clasp hook **(photo m)**.

## DESIGN ALTERNATIVES»

A single diamond focal turned on its side becomes a gorgeous pendant.

Frameless scrolls are lightweight yet substantial in a pair of statement earrings.

Eliminate the diamond frame, and make a swirling pendant with only a scroll center.

# Geometric Sliders

We delight in math marvels: the circle, the square, and the Reuleaux (a fat little triangle). The shapes we love are shown here as freely moving forms on a length of full Persian chain mail.

## MATERIALS

**wire**
- 53" (1.35m) 20-gauge, silver
- 36" (91.4cm) 20-gauge, gold
- 42" (1.07m) 30-gauge, gold

**jump rings**
- **680** (2 oz.) 4.8mm 20-gauge, gold

**tools**
- pliers kit
- ³/₄" (1.9cm) round mandrel (optional)

a

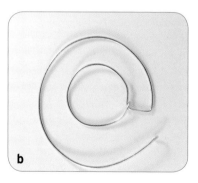
b

**MAKE THE PERSIAN CHAIN**

1 Make 28" (71cm) of **full Persian** chain mail (p. 102) using 4.8mm jump rings.

**MAKE THE CIRCLE**

2 Make a small open hook at the end of a 9" (23cm) piece of 20-gauge silver wire using the roundnose pliers' tips.

3 Form a ³/₄" (1.9cm) circle. Thread the working wire through the hook. Close the hook **(photo a)**.

4 Make a right-angle bend in the working wire so that this transition wire points away from the circle. Form a 1¼" (3.2cm) circle around the center circle **(photo b)**.

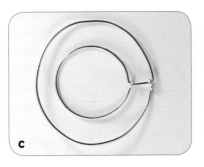

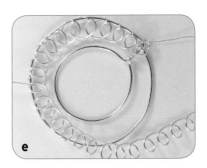

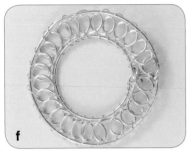

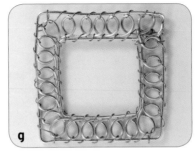

**5** Mark a point where the working wire crosses the transition wire. Cut the working wire 1/8" (3mm) beyond this mark. Make a hook in the end. Catch the very top of the outside bend with the hook. Close the hook **(photo c)**.

**6** Cut 12" (30cm) of 20-gauge silver wire, and make 5" (13cm) of 3/16" (5mm) **side-by-side loops (photo d)**. Position the loops around the frame opening with the base wire from the loop along the inner shape. Make a hook on the tail of the loop strand. Connect the hook as close to the center shape as possible. Close the hook.

**7** Stitch the side-by-side loops to the frame: Begin at the top of the transition wire. Cut a 14" (36cm) piece of 30-gauge wire, and leave a 1" tail. Go around the outer frame wire and back through a side-by-side loop top. Repeat, moving over one loop for each wrap **(photo e)**.

**8** Wrap the stitching wire once around the vertical transition frame piece. Stitch around the

center of the frame, around the back, and forward through the loop base. Move one loop at a time along the base and wrap all the way around the center frame element.

**9** Trim the loop strand base wire 1/8" beyond the last stitched loop. Make a hook in this wire. Catch the transition wire and close the hook.

**10** Twist the ends of the 30-gauge wire together and tuck them along the transition frame **(photo f)**.

**MAKE THE SQUARE**

**11** Cut a 9" (23cm) piece of 20-gauge silver wire, and make a small open hook at the end using the tips of the roundnose pliers. Mark four points spaced 3/4" (1.9cm) along the working wire. Use flatnose pliers to make a right-angle bend at each of the first three marks. Thread the working wire through the hook, and close the hook at the fourth mark.

**12** Mark 1/4" (6mm) from the hook along the transition

working wire to the larger square, and make a right-angle bend to place the working wire parallel to the center square. Mark at 1" (2.5cm). Bend at this point for the corner. Mark points from the bend at 1 1/4" (3.2cm), 2 1/2" (6.4cm), and 3 3/4" (9.5cm). Make consecutive right-angle bends at the marks.

**13** Repeat steps 5–10, using 20-gauge gold wire in step 6 to make the side-by-side loops to finish the square **(photo g)**.

**MAKE THE REULEAUX TRIANGLE**

**14** Make a small open hook at the end of a 9" (22.9cm) piece of 20-gauge silver wire using the tips of the roundnose pliers. Mark three 7/8" (2.2cm) lengths along the working wire. Use flatnose pliers to make a right-angle bend at each of the first three marks. String the working wire through the hook. Close the hook at the forth mark. Adjust the form by pulling out the centers of the edges to fatten them.

**15** Make a sharp-angled bend 3/8" (1cm) from the hook along the working wire to place the working wire parallel to the center triangle.

**16** Mark points from the bend at 1 3/8" (3.5cm), 2 3/4" (7cm), and 4 1/8" (10.5cm). Make consecutive right-angle bends at the marks. Adjust the form by pulling out the centers of the edges to fatten them, and space them at ¼" (6mm) from the inner triangle.

**17** Cut the working wire ⅛" beyond the last mark. Make a hook in the end. Catch the very top of the outside bend with the hook, and close the hook.

**18** Repeat steps 6-10, using 20-gauge gold wire in step 6 to make the side-by-side loops, to finish the triangle **(photo h)**.

### MAKE A CLASP

**19** Make a small open hook at the end of a 9" (21cm) piece of 20-gauge silver wire using the roundnose pliers' tips. Form a ¼" (6mm) circle. Thread the working wire through the hook. Close the hook.

**20** Make a right-angle bend in the working wire so that the transition wire points away from the circle. Mark a point ¼" beyond the circle. At a point ¾" (1.9cm) beyond the first mark, use roundnose pliers to make a tight U bend in the wire; this wire extension will be used for the hook.

**21** At the original ¼" mark, make a right-angle bend in the working wire so that the wire can now be used to make the outside of the frame. Form a ¾" circle around the center circle. At the point where the wire now crosses the hook extension, wrap the wire around the base of the hook extension three times, ending on the back.

**22** Make 3" (7.6cm) of ³⁄₁₆" (5mm) side-by-side loops with 20-gauge silver wire. Repeat steps 6-10. Make a **clasp hook** with the wire extension **(photo i)**.

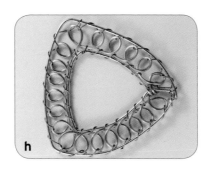

h

i

### ASSEMBLE THE NECKLACE

**23** Connect the two final rings on one end of the chain and the outside frame of the clasp with a ring.

**24** Attach a ring on the opposite end of the chain to act as the catch for the hook.

**25** String the geometric forms on the chain as desired.

If you would like the geometric forms to stay where you put them instead of moving freely, consider connecting the frames to the chain mail with rings.

### DESIGN ALTERNATIVE»

There are tons of possibilities for single shapes. We like these super-quick pairs of basic earrings.

# Three Wishes

Flowers, wine-colored sparkle, and the smooth harmony of European 4-in-1 chain mail pair with the graceful curves of compound wire in this lovely necklace. A closure with an encore flower is easy to make.

**MAKE HELM FLOWERS**

1 Make four **helm flowers** (p. 104) using 4.7mm (large) and 3.2mm (small) jump rings.

**MAKE EUROPEAN 4-IN-1 CHAIN MAIL PIECES**

2 Make two 7¼" (18.4cm) **European 4-in-1** chains (p. 101) using 4mm silver and gold jump rings.

**MAKE THE WISHBONES**

3 Cut two 14" (36cm), 12" (30cm), and 10" (25cm) pieces of 20-gauge round wire, and cut one of each length in 21-gauge twisted square wire. Stack the three 14" wires to create a compound wire, with a round wire on the bottom, the twisted square wire in the middle, and a round wire on the top. Repeat with the 12" and 10" wires.

**MATERIALS**

**wire**
- 82" (2.08m) 20-gauge, gold
- 41" (1.04m) 21-gauge twisted square, gold
- 18" (45.7cm) 21-gauge half-round, gold
- 30" (76.2cm) 30-gauge, gold

**jump rings**
- **340** (1.5 oz.) 4mm 18-gauge, silver
- **225** (1 oz.) 4mm 18-gauge, gold
- **72** 4.7mm 20-gauge, gold
- **48** 3.2mm 20-gauge, silver
- **4** 6mm sew-on prong-set rhinestones, garnet

**tools**
- pliers kit
- straight-edge ruler

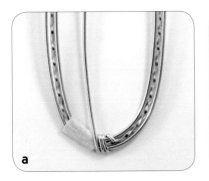

a

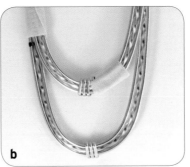

b

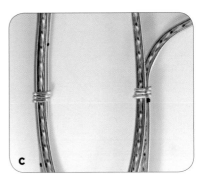

c

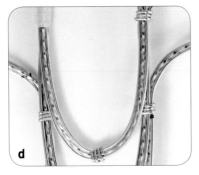

d

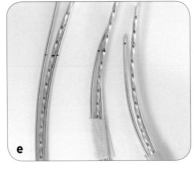

e

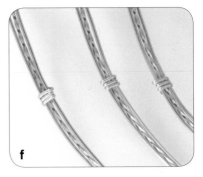

f

Each wire set will have the same initial bends. The wishbones' offset placement will allow you to make graduated curves. The lengths of the original wires differ, so when the compound wire sets are bound in place for the necklace, the final end wires will be nearly even.

All three wishbones are made the same way, except with successively longer ends (top to bottom). Mark both sides of each piece from the center front at 1¾" (4.4cm), 2" (5cm) (spread), and 4" (10cm) (decorative binding) before bending. For assembly, place each wishbone ¾" above the one below, as measured vertically from the center front, and connect each to the layer below with a binding wrap at the 1¾" marks on the lower wire.

4 Refer to the **figure** as you work. Mark a compound wire in the middle. Tape the wire near but offset from the respective center, making sure that all wires are flat and close together.

5 Use your fingers or nylon-jaw pliers to bend a curve that is 1" (2.5cm) wide, centering the mark at the bottom.

6 **Bind** the wire set with three wraps at the mark **(photo a)**.

7 Start with the top (10") wire set. At the 2" mark, gently pull the wire set out and down about halfway to horizontal, keeping the curves at a ¾" (1.9cm) radius. After making the curve, bind with three wraps at the 4" mark.

8 Repeat steps 4-7 with the two remaining wire sets.

9 Place the longest wire set on a flat surface. Stack the medium-length wire set on top, ¾" above the base set, by matching up the stacked wire sets at the 1¾" mark on the longest wire set **(photo b)**. Bind with three wraps around all six wires **(photo c)**.

10 Stack the shortest wire set on top, ¾" above the middle set. At the 1¾" mark on either side of the middle set, bind

with three wraps on each side around both wire sets **(photo d)**.

Because the first wire set has the outward curves made in step 6, it will be out of the way and not bound in when the top wire set is bound to the middle set.

11 Bend the ends of each side extension up in a wide curve. Adjust the curves until the ends of the three-sided piece fit within a ¾"-wide space. Lay a straight-edge ruler across all the ends, and mark them all the same length based on the shortest wire set **(photo e)**. Bind the ends with three wraps of half-round wire ⅛" (3mm) below the marks. Cut each set flush at the mark.

12 Secure and decorate each of the top two wishbone wire sets with additional bindings of three wire wraps. The wraps should be in line with the binding on the first and longest wishbone compound wire **(photo f)**.

13 Make another set of binding wire wraps at the ends of

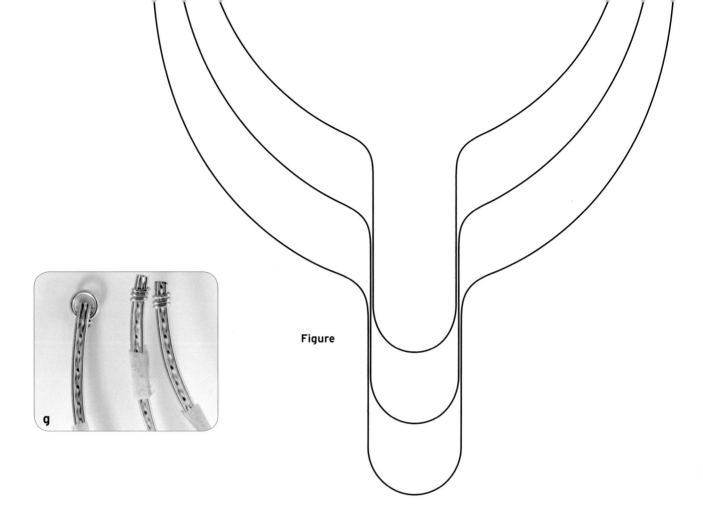

**Figure**

each compound wire set, stepping down ½" (1.3cm) from the end on the outside bundle, ¾" on the middle bundle, and 1" on the inside bundle.

**14** Use flatnose pliers to make a hook bend ¼" from the end of the inside wire set. String the top wrapped end through a 4mm ring. Compress the hook ends slightly. The wrapping wires next to the end will be hidden **(photo g)**.

Bending the compound wire at this point will place the wire wrap on the back of the piece where it will not be visible. Be careful not to slide the wraps off the end.

**MAKE A CLASP**

The clasp is made from two U-shaped connectors joined together.

**15** Cut two 2½" (6.4cm) pieces of 20-gauge round wire and one 2½" piece of twisted square wire. Make a compound wire as in step 3. Stack in this order: round wire, twisted square wire, and round wire.

**16** Wrap the compound wire with tape to secure on one end, and gently bend it into a flat U shape. The U should fit in a ¾"-wide space. Bind the bundle with three wraps within ⅛" of the end of the shortest wire on both sides.

Bending the bundle into a U shape will cause the wires to move, which will make the ends uneven.

Trim the ends so they are even with the length of the shortest wire.

**17** Use flatnose pliers to make a U bend in the end of the

wire set below the wraps. String the top wrapped end through a 4mm ring. Roll the ends of the wire toward the wire set. Compress the whole connection slightly. The wrapping wires next to the end will be hidden. Repeat for the bottom end.

**18** Repeat steps 15-17 to make a second U-shaped connector.

**19** Connect the top of the U shape to the opposite side of the ring from the first U connector. Attach the bottom of the new U to the bottom ring from the first connector.

Use colored rings to create a stunning scarf ring.

Capture a helm flower in a small wishbone loop for a pretty pendant.

A smaller version of this project makes a bangle bracelet.

**MAKE TWO T-SHAPED HOOKS**

**20** Cut a 2½" piece of 20-gauge round wire, and make a small hook on one end. Face the hook to the back of the work. Mark a point ³⁄₈" along the wire, and make a U bend.

**21** Use roundnose pliers to make a small loop as close to the bend as possible. Make a second loop directly below the end of the hook. Make a third loop ¼" further down the wire.

**22** Make a U-shaped bend as close to the last loop as possible. ³⁄₈" from that bend, use flatnose pliers to make a sharp bend in the working wire away from the work. ³⁄₄" (1.9cm) from that bend, make a sharp U bend, bringing the working wire back toward the initial hook.

**23** Trim the wire to ⅛", and make a hook on the end. Connect this hook with the initial hook. Close and compress both hooks. The piece will look like an open T frame **(photo h)**.

**24** Cut a 1½" piece of twisted square wire to make the hook insert. Bend the wire in half, and compress. Bend each wire end at a right angle ³⁄₈" from the end **(photo i)**.

**25** Place the twisted square wire T into the open T frame. Bind the wire to the frame with three wraps on either side between the loops and on the long extension ¼" from the end **(photo j)**. Place the T down, with the front side up. Use roundnose pliers to make a hook (make sure you include the square twisted wire in this bend). Repeat steps 20–25 to make a second hook.

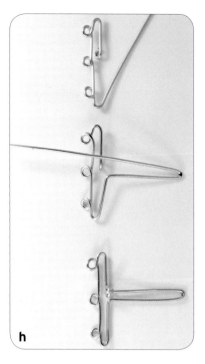

h

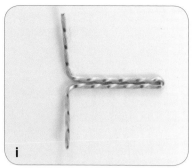

i

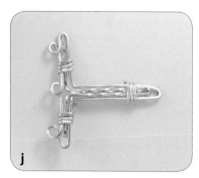

j

k

l

m

n

## ASSEMBLE THE NECKLACE

**26** Connect a rhinestone to the center of each helm flower: String a 2" (5cm) piece of 24-gauge wire through one set of holes in the rhinestone. Go through a pair of back small rings on each side of the flower, twist both wire ends together on the back, and tuck them out of the way.

**27** Connect the top of a wishbone to the left-end ring on the outside row of a piece of European 4-in-1 chain mail with a 4mm ring. Repeat with the center row and the right-end ring **(photo k)**. Repeat on the other end of the necklace.

**28** Attach the clasp hook: Slide the final end rings on the top back of the European 4-in-1 (left, right, and center) through the coil loops on the T-bar clasp **(photo l)**. Repeat on the other end of the necklace with the other half of the clasp.

**29** Connect a hook to the center double U. Close

the hook so it will not come off. Connect the second hook to the opposite side of the double U. Do not close this hook.

**30** Attach the back top of a helm flower to the double U section of the clasp **(photo m)**: Connect a small back double silver ring in the helm flower and the ring that the two U sections are attached to with a small ring. Repeat at the bottom.

**31** Attach the remaining three helm flowers to the front of the necklace. Each flower is attached to the low curve of the compound wire at the center. Cut 3" (7.6cm) of half-round wire, and string one end of the wire

through a pair of small rings on the center back of a helm flower. String the other end of the wire through a pair of small rings on the opposite side of the flower. Carefully wrap the end of the wire around the wishbone compound wire set at the base of the curve three times to bind it. Compress, and trim the excess wire. Repeat for the other wire end. Attach the remaining two helm flowers in a similar fashion, binding them individually to each remaining wishbone **(photo n)**.

# CHAPTER 5

# Branch & Wrap

# Spider Mums

These lively little flowers float freely around your wrist. The blossom link has an open center, and the mini box chain mail makes the perfect willowy stem. Using one of the flower petals to make the clasp hook means this bracelet will always have its best face forward.

## MATERIALS

**wire**
- 32" (81cm) 20-gauge, gold
- 32" 24-gauge, gold

**jump rings**
- **225** (1 oz.) 4.7mm
  20-gauge, gold

**tools**
- pliers kit
- sharpened dowel
  (optional)

### MAKE BOX CHAIN MAIL

**1** Make three 2" (5cm) pieces of **box chain** (p. 97) using 4.7mm jump rings.

### MAKE THE SPIDER MUMS

**2** Make a small hook on the end of the 20-gauge wire with the tip of roundnose pliers. Mark 20 points 3/8" (1cm) from this loop.

**3** Begin at the first mark, and make a series of 3/8" petals by bending the wire alternately down and up along the wire at each mark with roundnose pliers **(photo a)**.

**4** At the bottom end of the tenth petal, bend the working wire end out at a right angle to the row of petals.

**5** Using flatnose pliers, compress each petal to make them uniformly thick from the rounded top to the base **(photo b)**. Trim the end, leaving 1/4" (6mm). Bend the end into a hook.

**6** Form the petals into a circle. Connect both hook ends, and squeeze the hooks shut. Align this closure as close to the bottom of the other petal bases as you can **(photo c)**.

**7** Cut 32" (81cm) of 24-gauge wire to make the wrapped center: String the wire up through the center opening, leaving a 1" (2.5cm) tail. Lay the wrapping wire across the base of the petals. Wrap over three petals in a counter-clockwise direction. Pull the wire to the back. Bring the wire back toward the starting position for two petals **(photo d)**. Come up between the petals and continue wrapping counter-clockwise—over three and back two—until you've circled the flower. Repeat the wrapping sequence for a fuller flower.

**8** Bring the end of the working wire to the back. Find the original end, and twist the two together. Trim and bend the ends to align with the wrapping wires. To make the inside hole more uniform, use a sharpened dowel or pencil, and twist it gently in the opening.

**9** To give the flowers a livelier look, press the petal bases nearest the center down on a flat surface. This will make the petals "pop." Gently pull the petals up to cup the flower center. If desired, use your fingers or roundnose pliers to roll the tips of each petal back down.

### MAKE A SPIDER MUM CLASP

**10** Repeat steps 2 and 3, stopping after the ninth petal.

**11** After the bottom end of the ninth petal, extend the wire out to 1" and then back (this extension will become the closure hook). At the base of the extension, bend the wire end out at a right angle to the row of petals.

**12** Repeat steps 5-9, except do not shape the wire extension **(photo e)**.

**13** With the front of the flower facing up, use roundnose pliers to roll up the tip of the long petal **(photo f)**. Flip the flower over. Bend the rolled tip back toward the flower, making a hook **(photo g)**. Match the curve of the back of the hook to the flower.

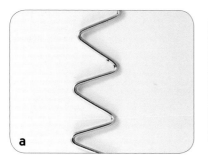

a

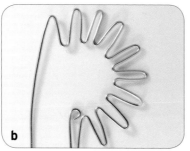

b

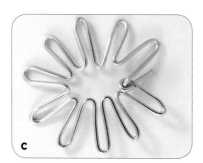

c

d

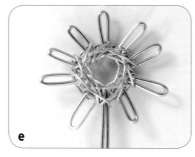

e

f

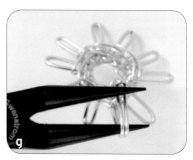

g

### ASSEMBLE THE BRACELET

**14** Lay out alternating pieces of spider mums and box chain. Place the clasp at one end. Connect both end rings of the box chain to an open petal on a spider mum. Attach the opposite end of the box chain to the second spider mum the same way. Repeat for the final spider mum and the clasp.

**15** On the bracelet end opposite the clasp, connect two rings to the final two rings of the chain to serve as the catch for the clasp hooks.

Adjust the length of the box chain mail sections for a shorter or longer bracelet.

# Squares & Lace

Made with alternating wire-wrapped
squares and chain mail lace designs, this
stunning gold-and-silver bracelet is a go-to
piece for dressing up or going casual.
The clasp is a clever variation of the
wrapped square and hides in plain sight
for an almost invisible connection.

## MAKE THE CHAIN MAIL

**1** Make four squares of **Victorian
lace** (p. 106) using 3mm
jump rings.

## MAKE SQUARE WIRE COMPONENTS

**2** Cut a 10" (25cm) piece of
20-gauge wire, and make a
small loop at one end.

**3** Adjust the loop and wire
so that the working wire is
positioned vertically from the
center of the loop. Measure and
mark a point 1" (2.5cm) beyond

## MATERIALS

### wire
- 42" (74cm) 20-gauge, gold
- 280" (7.11m) 24-gauge,
  gold

### jump rings
- **210** (1.7 oz.) 3mm
  18-gauge, sterling silver
- **6** 6mm 16-gauge, sterling
  silver

### tools
- pliers kit

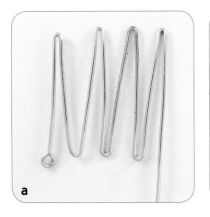

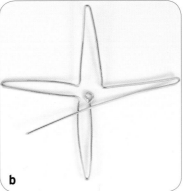

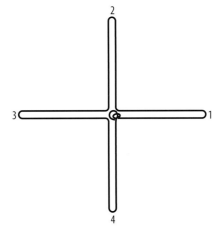

**Figure 1**

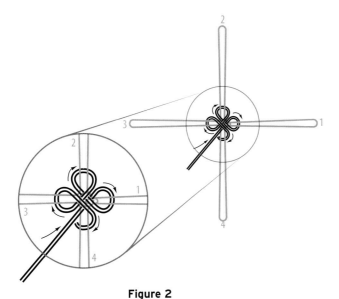

**Figure 2**

the loop. Using flatnose pliers, bend the wire sharply down to make a peak. Mark a point 1" after the peak, and make a sharp bend up, creating a valley. Repeat this series of bends twice. Mark a point 1" after the final valley, and make a sharp bend down, creating the last peak for a total of four peaks and three valleys **(photo a)**.

4 Close each peak so the wires are parallel and side by side without gaps, and compress the wires to make four branches. Pull these tightly compressed branches around until they are each at right angles to each other and form a cross frame encircling the loop **(photo b)**.

5 To complete the frame and get rid of the wire ends, leave ⅛" (3mm) on the working wire for a hook, and trim. Make a small hook, and connect it to the initial loop. Squeeze the hook closed. Trim any excess wire **(photo c)**.

6 Place the frame wire in position with branches pointing up, down, left, and right. Branch #1 is at the right. Branches #2, #3, and #4 follow counter-clockwise **(figure 1)**.

In the next step, you will complete wraps on the front

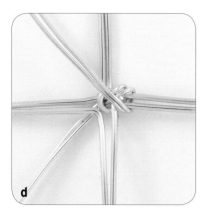

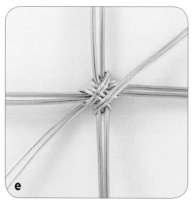

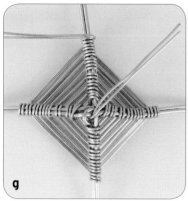

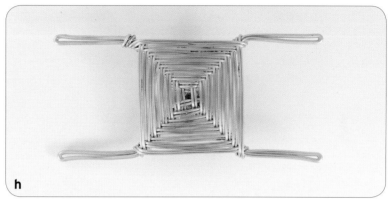

of the link to create a God's eye. Keep the link front facing you. Use your thumb or nylon-jaw pliers to maintain even tension and alignment with each wrap.

**7** Cut a 70" (1.78m) piece of 24-gauge wire, and fold it in half. You will use this wire doubled to wrap the square.

Keep the doubled wires straight, close, and parallel. Make sure they don't twist as you work.

**8** With the doubled wire, come up through the center loop of the frame and leave a 1" tail. Wrap as follows (refer to **figure 2**):

**Layer 1:** Go down in the space between branch #1 and #2. Go around the back of #1 and come up between #1 and #4. Go across between #2 and #3 **(photo d)**. Go around the back of #2 and

come up between #2 and #1. Go across between #3 and #4. Go around the back of #3 and come up between #2 and #3. Go across between #1 and #4, go down between #1 and #4, and come up in the space between between #4 and #3. Go over #4 and #1 **(photo e)**.

**Layer 2:** Go down between #1 and #2. Wrap around the back of #1 and come up between #1 and #4. Go over #1 and #2, and go down between #2 and #3. Wrap around the back of #2 and go up between #2 and #1. Go over #2 and #3, and go down between #3 and #4. Wrap around the back of #3, and go up between #2 and #3. Go over #3 and #4. Go around the back of #4, come up between #3 and #4, and go over #4 and #1.

Repeat layer 2 to make eight layers, with each layer resting next to and outside the previous layer.

The pattern is: Cross over two branches, go down, and make a full wrap around the second.

**9** To end the wrapping, make one additional wrap with the 24-gauge wire around branch #1 **(photos f and g)**. End at the back, and trim any excess wire.

**10** Twist the original tail ends together. Leave enough length to tuck the ends into the back. Trim any excess wire.

The branch ends still project about ⅜–½" (1–1.3cm) beyond the wrappings. This may vary a bit in length, depending on your wrapping tension.

**11** To make these branch ends into connecting links, use chainnose pliers held flat across the branch to bend the branch extensions to each side while keeping the wires even, parallel,

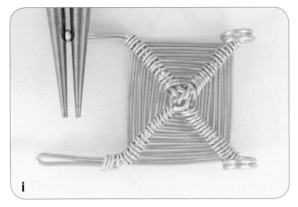

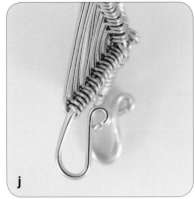

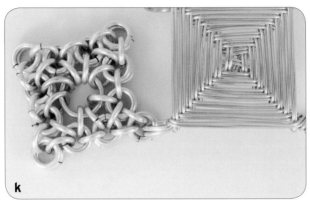

and untwisted. Bend a top and bottom branch to the right. Bend a top and bottom branch to the left. The branch ends should be down far enough so they are in line with the side wrapping wires **(photo h, p. 83)**.

**12** Turn the square to the back. Roll the branch extensions into loops using roundnose pliers **(photo i)**.

**13** Repeat steps 2–12 for a total of three square components.

**MAKE A DOUBLE-HOOK CLASP**
Make a small adjustment to the branch dimensions for a clasp; two consecutive branches need to be ½" longer.

**14** Make a small loop at the tail end of a 12" (30cm) piece of the 20-gauge wire. Adjust the loop and wire so the working wire is positioned vertically from the center of the loop.

**15** Measure 1½" (3.8cm) beyond the loop, and bend the wire sharply down to make a peak. 1½" after the first bend, make a second sharp bend up to make a valley. Repeat to make two branches that are 1½" long.

**16** Measure 1" beyond the valley, and bend the wire sharply down, making a peak. 1" after the peak bend, make a second sharp bend up to make a valley. 1" beyond the valley, make a sharp bend down for a final (fourth) peak.

**17** Compress the wires of each of the four peaks tightly, keeping the wires flat and parallel. Pull these compressed branches around to form a cross.

**18** Leave ⅛" on the working wire to make a small hook, and connect it to the initial wire loop. Wrap the piece with doubled 24-gauge wire as in step 8.

**19** To make the hooks, use chainnose pliers to bend the branch extensions to each side. The two long branches must go to the same side, and the two short branches will go to the side opposite. Bend the branch ends down far enough so they are in line with the side wrapping wires.

**20** With the front of the square facing up, use roundnose pliers to roll up just the tip of each branch extension. Flip the square over. Use round-nose pliers to bend back the wires

³/₈" from the rolled tips, making a hook. Repeat with the other extension to make a second parallel hook **(photo j)**.

**21** While still on the square back, roll the two short branch extensions into loops using roundnose pliers. Each loop should touch the back of the link.

**ASSEMBLE THE BRACELET**

**22** Lay out the pieces, alternating a square wire component with a chain mail square. Place the double-hook clasp with the hook facing away from the other pieces.

**23** Connect the top branch of a square wire component to the corner rings of a chain mail square by gently opening the wire loops just enough to slide in a square ring. Tighten the loops by rolling the branch tip back around into a loop and pushing it into contact with the back of the square **(photo k)**.

**24** Connect the bottom branch on the same side to the bottom corner ring on the chain mail square. Repeat on the other side of the square. Add alternating pieces until all six square wire components and chain mail squares are attached.

**25** Connect the double-hook clasp using the two short branch extensions that were

# DESIGN ALTERNATIVE»

Make small square wire components for a sweet pair of dangles.

rolled into loops: Open them just enough to slide in a ring, and then roll the branch tip back around into a loop. Repeat for the bottom connector.

The hooks connect with the free corner rings of the final lace ring on the opposite side of the bracelet. For a slightly longer bracelet, add sets of two rings to each corner.

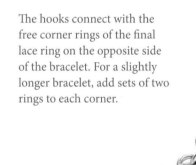

# Dragon Pillows

This stunning bracelet provides dimensions tall and deep. High wire-wrapped domes alternate with deep dragonscale chain mail. The clasp is a clever variation of the wrapped dome. The hooks tuck underneath the square and attach to a side bar with a slim profile that hides in plain sight.

## DRAGONSCALE CHAIN MAIL

1 Make four 1" pieces of **dragonscale** chain mail (p. 100) using 6mm (large) and 4mm (small) jump rings.

## MAKE THE SQUARE FRAME

2 Use roundnose pliers to make a small loop at the end of a 10" (25cm) piece of 20-gauge wire.

3 Adjust the loop and wire so that the working wire is positioned vertically from the center of the loop. Mark a point 1" (2.5cm) beyond the loop. Using flatnose pliers, bend the wire sharply down to make a peak.

1" after the first peak, make a second sharp bend up to create a

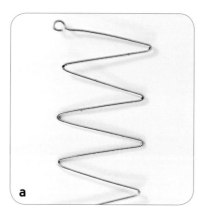

a

valley. Repeat this series of bends twice. 1" after the final valley, make a sharp bend down to create the last peak. There will be a series of four peaks **(photo a)**.

## MATERIALS

**wire**
- 46" (1.17m) 20-gauge, gold
- 4" (10.2cm) 21-gauge half-round, silver
- 280" (7.11m) 24-gauge, gold colored

**jump rings**
- **160** (1 oz.) 6mm 18-gauge, gold color
- **160** (1 oz.) 4mm 18-gauge, silver color

**tools**
- pliers kit

b

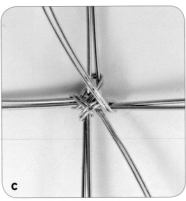

c

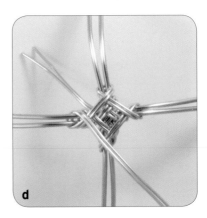

d

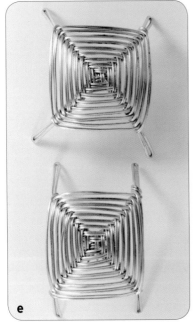

e

4 Close each of the four peaks so that the wires are side by side without gaps. Compress the wires so they make four branches. Pull these tightly compressed branches around until they are at right angles to each other and form a cross frame encircling the loop. Trim the working wire, leaving 1/8" (3mm) to make a small hook with the roundnose pliers' tips. Connect the hook through the initial wire loop. Squeeze the hook closed **(photo b)**.

**WRAP THE DOMES**

Use your thumb to push the tips of the branch wires down and create a domed shape. Retain this shape, adjusting after each wrap row if necessary. The finished link will fit in a 1" square.

5 Position the domed wire frame as in **figure 1**, p. 82, to begin a God's eye. Branch #1 is at the right, and branches #2, #3, and #4 follow counter-clockwise, and the wraps are done on the front of the link. Use your thumb or nylon-jaw pliers to maintain even tension and alignment with each wrap.

6 Fold a 70" (1.78m) piece of 24-gauge wire in half, and use it doubled. Keep the double wires straight, close, and parallel, and make sure that they do not twist. Leave a 1" tail at the open end of the double wrapping wire, and string this tail through the center frame loop to the back.

The 1" tail is pulled to hang down after this first row of wraps and is not wrapped into future rows.

**Layer 1:** Go down in the space between branch #1 and #2. Go around the back of #1 and come up between #1 and #4. Go across between #2 and #3. Go around the back of #2 and come up between #2 and #1. Go across between #3 and #4. Go around the back of #3 and come up between #2 and #3. Go across between #1 and #4, go down

between #1 and #4, and come up in the space between between #4 and #3. Go over #4 and #1.

**Layer 2:** Go down between #1 and #2. Wrap around the back of #1 **(photo c)**, and come up between #1 and #4. Go over #1 and #2, and go down between #2 and #3. Wrap around the back of #2 and go up between #2 and #1. Go over #2 and #3, and go down between #3 and #4. Wrap around the back of #3, and go up between #2 and #3 **(photo d)**. Go over #3 and #4. Go around the back of #4, come up between #3 and #4, and go over #4 and #1.

Repeat layer 2 to make eight layers, with each layer resting next to and outside the previous layer.

The pattern is: Cross over two branches, go down, and make a full wrap around the second.

7 To end the wrapping, make one additional wrap with the 24-gauge wire around the last branch. End at the back, and trim any excess wire.

8 Twist the ends of the original tail together. Leave enough length to tuck the ends into the back. Trim any excess.

The branch ends still project about 3/8– 1/2" (1–1.3cm) beyond the wrappings.

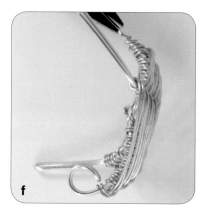

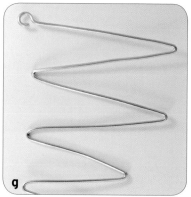

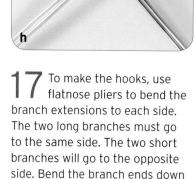

**9** To make these branch ends into connecting links, pull the extensions to reach right and left in line with the horizontal wrap **(photo e)**. On the back of the square, roll the branch extensions toward the corners into loops using roundnose pliers **(photo f)**.

### MAKE A SQUARE CONNECTOR DOUBLE-HOOK CLASP

Create a hooked closure by making a small adjustment to the square frame branch dimensions. Two consecutive branches need to be 3/8" (1cm) longer.

**10** Make a small loop at the tail end of a 12" (30.5cm) piece of the wire to use later. Adjust the loop and wire so that the working wire is positioned vertically from the center of the loop.

**11** 1 3/8" (3.5cm) beyond the loop, bend the wire sharply down to make a peak. 1 3/8" after the first bend, make a second sharp bend up to make a valley. Repeat to make two 1 3/8"-long branches.

**12** 1" beyond the valley, bend the wire sharply down to make a peak. 1" after the peak, bend, make a second sharp bend up to make a valley. 1" beyond the valley, make a sharp bend down to make a final (fourth) peak **(photo g)**.

**13** Compress the wires of each of the four peaks tightly, keeping the wires flat and parallel. Pull these tightly compressed branches around at right angles to each other until they form a cross.

**14** To complete the frame, leave 1/8" on the working wire to make a small hook with the tips of the roundnose pliers.

**15** Curl the hook through the wire loop. Squeeze the hook closed **(photo h)**.

**16** Repeat steps 6-8 **(photo i, p. 90)**.

**17** To make the hooks, use flatnose pliers to bend the branch extensions to each side. The two long branches must go to the same side. The two short branches will go to the opposite side. Bend the branch ends down far enough so they are in line with the side wrapping wires.

**18** With the front of the square facing up, use roundnose pliers to roll up just the tip of each of the long hook extensions. Flip the square over. Use roundnose pliers to bend back the wires at a point 3/8" back from the rolled tips, making a hook. This design makes two parallel hooks.

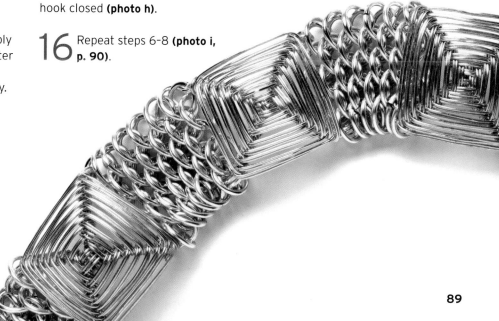

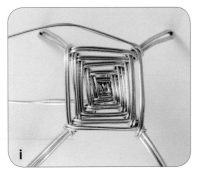

i

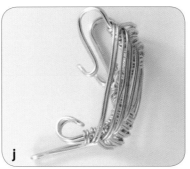

j

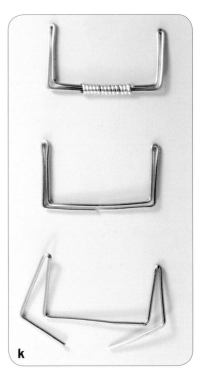

k

l

m

**19** While still on the square back, roll the two short branch extensions into loops using roundnose pliers. Each loop should touch the back of the link **(photo j)**.

**MAKE THE CLASP BAR**

**20** Cut 4" (7.6cm) of 20-gauge wire. Use flatnose pliers to make a U shape: Bend ½" of the ends up at right angles, leaving a ⅞" (2.2cm) wide wire middle.

**21** On one end, use roundnose pliers to make a small U-turn and bring the working end down along the outside of the form. At the corner, bend the wire to follow the base of the original U. Repeat on the other end.

**22** Carefully trim the ends so they match up near the center of the form.

**23** Use 21-gauge half-round silver wire to wrap the form, starting ¼" (6mm) to one side of the matched wire ends. Wrap over the cut and ¼" beyond. Compress tightly **(photo k)**.

**24** Using roundnose pliers, roll each wire extension into a loop **(photo l)**.

Because the clasp hooks fit within the bar opening, they will not slide. This gives the bracelet a continuous flow and makes the clasp nearly invisible.

**ASSEMBLE THE BRACELET**

**25** Lay out alternating domes and dragonscale chain mail pieces. Place the dome with the hook on the end.

**26** Gently unroll a formed branch loop on a dome just enough to slide into the closest gold ring from the chain mail. Close the loop. Repeat at the top and bottom until all of the domes and chain mail pieces are connected **(photo m)**.

**27** Attach the clasp bar to the end of the bracelet opposite the dome with the hooks: Gently unroll the clasp bar end loop just enough to slide into the closest gold ring from the chain mail.

# Byzantine Waterfall

This necklace is a triple treat of deep triangular elements attached to that favorite weave of texture and form: a Byzantine rope. The chain mail rope combines alternating gold and silver for an even more upscale look. The clasp is both useful and subtle: a decorated hook and eye nestled into the rope.

## MATERIALS

**wire**
- 30" (76cm) 20-gauge, gold
- 324" (8.23m) 24-gauge, gold

**jump rings**
- **345** (3 oz.) 4.5mm 16-gauge, gold
- **425** (3 oz.) 4.5mm 16-gauge, silver
- **2** 4.5mm 20-gauge, silver

- **3** 6mm, prong-set, sew-on rhinestones, clear

**tools**
- pliers kit

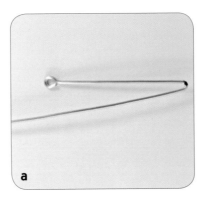
a

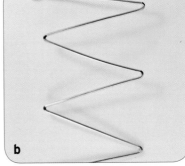
b

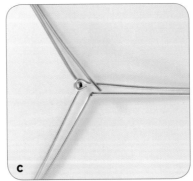
c

d

**MAKE BYZANTINE CHAIN MAIL ROPE**

**1** Make two 14" (36cm) pieces of **Byzantine** chain mail (p. 97) using 4.5mm 16-gauge silver and gold jump rings.

**MAKE DEEP TRIANGLES**

**2** Use roundnose pliers to make a small loop at the tail end of an 8" (21cm) piece of 20-gauge wire.

**3** Adjust the loop and wire so the working wire is positioned vertically from the center of the loop. 1¼" (3.2cm) beyond the loop, use flatnose pliers to bend the wire sharply down and make a peak **(photo a)**. 1¼" (3.2cm) after the first peak, make a second sharp bend up to create a valley. Repeat this series of bends twice to make three peaks and two valleys **(photo b)**.

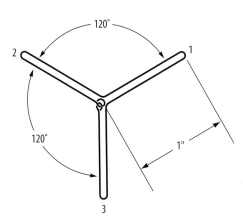

**Figure 1**

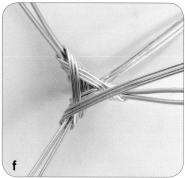

**Figure 2**

4 Close each peak so the wires are parallel and side by side without gaps. Compress the wires to make three branches.

5 Pull these tightly compressed branches around until they are evenly spaced 120 degrees from each other **(photo c)**.

6 Trim the working end, leaving 1/8" (3mm) on the wire. Make a small hook with the tips of the roundnose pliers.

7 Connect the hook to the beginning wire loop. Squeeze the hook closed **(photo d)**.

**WRAP THE TRIANGLES**

8 Place the frame wire in position with branches pointing left, right, and down. Branch #1 is at the right, and branches #2 and #3 follow counter-clockwise **(figure 1)**. Bend the branches up so the tips are higher than the center.

Complete these wraps on the front of the link. Keep the link front facing you and use your thumb or nylon-jaw pliers to maintain even tension and alignment.

9 Cut three 30" (76cm) pieces of 24-gauge wire. This wire will wrap around the branches of the triangle piece frame.

Keep the triple wires straight, close, and parallel, and make sure that they do not twist. Tape each end to prevent the wires from twisting.

10 With the triple wire, come up through the center loop of the frame, leaving a 1" tail. Wrap as follows (refer to **figure 2**):

**Layer 1:** Go down between #2 and #1. Go around the back of #1 and up between #1 and #3 **(photo e)**. Bring the wires across to the space between #2 and #3. Go around the back of #2 and come up between #2 and #1. Go over #2 and #3, go around #3, and come up between #3 and #2. Go over #1 **(photo f)**. Repeat eight times.

This piece requires nine layers of wraps. Keep the branches straight, bent slightly upward, and equally spaced at 120 degrees to each other. Keep the triple wrap smooth and straight.

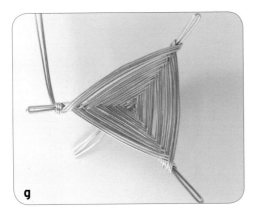

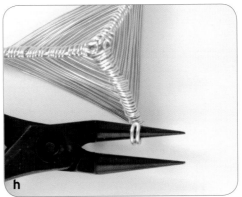

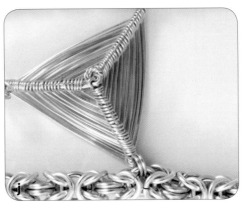

**11** To finish, make an additional wrap with the 24-gauge wires around the last branch **(photo g)**. End at the back, and trim any excess wire.

**12** Twist the ends of the original wire tail together. Leave enough length to tuck the ends into the back. Trim any excess wire.

The branch ends still project about ³/₈–¹/₂" (1–1.3cm) beyond the wrappings. This will vary a bit in length, as each person uses slightly different wrapping tension.

**13** To make a connecting link, use chainnose pliers held flat across the branch to bend the branch extensions to each side while keeping the wires even, parallel, and untwisted. Bend

the top right branch down to horizontal right. Bend a top left branch down to horizontal left. (You don't need to adjust the branch pointing down.)

**14** Turn the triangle to the back. Roll the branch extensions into rings using roundnose pliers **(photo h)**. Repeat to make two more triangles.

**MAKE THE CLASP**

**15** The clasp for this necklace is a hook and ring. Connect a gold ring to the end of one Byzantine chain.

**16** For the hook, cut 6" (15cm) of 20-gauge wire, and bend it in half. Use roundnose pliers to bend up the folded tip and complete a **clasp hook**.

**17** String a rhinestone on the wires, and turn it to face out. Use roundnose pliers to make an open loop below the rhinestone. String both ends of the wire through a closed 4.5mm gold ring. Slide the ring down to rest in the open loop. Bring the ends of the wires back toward the hook. Use one wire to make two wraps on one side of the rhinestone, and use the other wire to make two wraps on the other side **(photo i)**.

**ASSEMBLE THE NECKLACE**

**18** Connect the triangles to the chain mail ropes 1¹/₂" (3.8cm), 3¹/₂" (8.9cm), and 5¹/₂" (14cm) from the bottom of each chain. Connect the rolled loops of the branch extensions to a double set of rings in the rope **(photo j)**.

k

19 Connect the base of the rhinestone and the last two end rings of the rope with a 20-gauge ring **(photo k)**.

20 Connect the clasp hook to the last two gold rings on the rope.

21 Connect a 4.5mm 20-gauge silver jump ring to the last two gold rings on the other end of the necklace. The clasp hook will catch this final ring.

## DESIGN ALTERNATIVES»

Make an earring with simple Byzantine topped with a gemstone drop for sparkle.

Wire a crystal to a component for a chic, glittering pendant.

Make a loop of Byzantine chain mail for a new twist on hoop earrings.

# Technique Reference

# Chain Mail Techniques

**Figure 1**

**Figure 2**

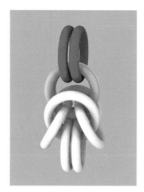

**Figure 3**

**Figure 4**

## BOX CHAIN

**1.** Follow steps 1-4 of the Byzantine chain mail weave (below).
**2.** Slide two open rings into the flipped rings, following the path illustrated in step 4 of "Byzantine." These two rings are the first of the two sets you will add for the next box flip **(FIGURE 1)**.
**3.** Connect a second pair of rings to the pair added in the step 2 **(FIGURES 2 AND 3)**.
**4.** Flip one top ring to the left and the other top ring to the right **(FIGURE 4)**.
**5.** Repeat steps 2-4 until you reach the desired length.

## BYZANTINE

Byzantine forms the basis for many other weaves.

**1.** Close two rings. Slide an open ring through the two closed rings, and close the ring. Slide another open ring through the same two closed rings, and close the ring. Slide two more open rings through the two rings just added, and close the rings. This is a 2-in-2-in-2 chain **(FIGURE 1)**.
**2.** Hold the chain segment vertically **(FIGURE 2)**. If desired, add a twist tie or paper clip to the end rings to hold on as you weave.
**3.** Using your thumbnail, hold the two end rings against your index finger. Note how the second set of rings stands straight up in the air and the third set of rings flops over. Flip one ring to the right and one ring to the left **(FIGURE 3)**.
**4.** Spread the middle two rings apart, revealing the two rings beneath them **(FIGURE 4)**. Slide a

**Figure 1**

**Figure 2**

**Figure 3**

**Figure 4**

toothpick underneath the bottoms of those rings, and lift to open a space, if needed.

**Figure 5**    **Figure 6**    **Figure 7**

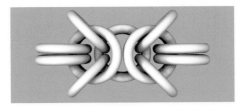

**Figure 8**

**5.** Slide two new rings into the two exposed rings. These two rings are the first of the three sets you will add for the next Byzantine flip **(FIGURE 5)**.

The two rings added to the Byzantine flip are called "connector rings." The rest of the rings are called "main rings." Projects with two ring colors will specify which rings are which.

**6.** Slide two new rings into the rings added in the previous step **(FIGURE 6)**.

**7.** Connect two new rings to the rings added in step 6 **(FIGURE 7)**.

Make sure that you count the two rings added in step 5 as the first set of three.

**8.** Repeat steps 3-7 (the Byzantine flip). This completes one full segment of Byzantine **(FIGURE 8)**.

**9.** Repeat steps 6-8 until you reach the desired length.

---

## DIAGONAL BYZANTINE

**1.** For this project, you'll need large, medium, and small rings. First, create a center segment: Make one full Byzantine segment with small rings. Turn the segment so that the connector rings (shown in red) are at the top and the bottom. Spread them out to open a space between the connector rings **(FIGURE 1)**.

**2.** Slide an open large ring between the connector rings on the top, and close. Slide an open medium ring through the connector rings on the bottom, and close **(FIGURE 2)**.

**3.** Repeat steps 1 and 2 for the remaining segments, using only medium rings in step 2.

**4.** Turn the center segment around so the large and medium rings look like donuts **(FIGURE 3)**.

**5.** Open the large ring at the top of the center segment, slide it into the two middle side rings in another segment, and close. Open the medium ring at the bottom of that segment, slide it into the two middle side rings in the center segment, and close **(FIGURE 4)**.

**6.** Continue adding segments on both sides of the center segment until you reach the desired length **(FIGURE 5)**.

**Figure 1**

**Figure 2**

**Figure 3**

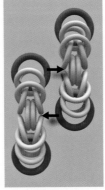

**Figure 4**

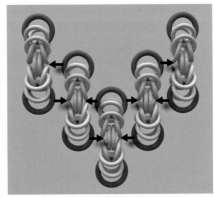

**Figure 5**

# DOUBLE HALF PERSIAN

**1.** These instructions refer to rings by number as they are added (they will all be the same size). Lay out two closed rings (ring 1 and ring 2), with the left ring overlapping the right ring to create an "eye" where the two rings intersect **(FIGURE 1)**. To help keep track of the rings as you weave, put a twist tie on the bottom of each ring. Make the twist tie on the right shorter, and always keep it on the right side as you weave.

**2.** Insert an open ring 3 through the "eye," and close the ring **(FIGURE 2)**.

**3.** Push ring 3 down and to the left from a vertical to a horizontal position **(FIGURE 3)**.

**4.** Insert an open ring 4 around the outside of the eye **(FIGURE 4)**.

**5.** Grasp rings 3 and 4, and push them down so they change from a horizontal to a vertical position. (For all other rows, push the newly added rings up.) Your work now looks like the original two overlapping rings, but this time the right ring is overlapping the left ring. The overlap creates an "eye" in the middle of the two rings. The right/left overlapping will alternate with each new row **(FIGURE 5)**.

**6.** Insert an open ring 5 through the "eye" created by the overlapping rings 3 and 4 **(FIGURE 6)**.

**7.** Push ring 5 down and to the left from a vertical to a horizontal position **(FIGURE 7)**.

**8.** Insert an open ring 6 around the outside of the eye **(FIGURE 8)**.

**9.** With each new row, change the orientation of your work. Grasp the last two rings added (5 and 6), and push them up so that they are in a vertical position, presenting an "eye" for the next ring. Rings 3 and 4 are in a horizontal position **(FIGURE 9)**.

**10.** Insert an open ring 7 through the "eye" created by the overlapping rings 5 and 6 **(FIGURE 10)**.

**11.** Push ring 7 down and to the left from a vertical to a horizontal position. Slide ring 8 around the outside of the eye **(FIGURE 11)**. After pushing rings 7 and 8 from a horizontal to a vertical position, you will be ready to add the next row.

The key to understanding this weave is "flipping up" the last two rings added so that you can see the "hole" and are ready to add the next row. First, the hole is visible, ready for the next two rings. Next, two new rings have been added and lie in the horizontal position. Lastly, the two rings added have been pushed up to the vertical position and the hole is visible **(FIGURE 12)**.

**12.** Continue adding new rows until the piece reaches the desired length.

**Figure 1**

**Figure 2**

**Figure 3**

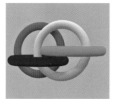

**Figure 4**

**Figure 5**

**Figure 6**

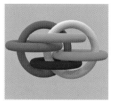

**Figure 7**

**Figure 8**

**Figure 9**

**Figure 10**

**Figure 11**

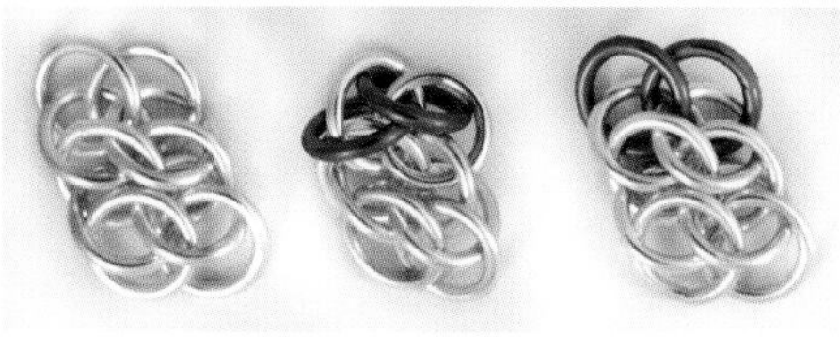

**Figure 12**

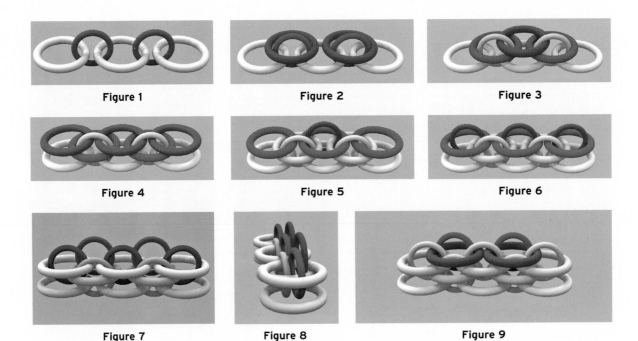

Figure 1

Figure 2

Figure 3

Figure 4

Figure 5

Figure 6

Figure 7

Figure 8

Figure 9

# DRAGONSCALE

This weave is constructed with large and small rings. Large rings only go through small rings, and small rings only go through large rings. Rows are built vertically on top of each other and stretch out to form the flat length of the dragonscale chain.

**1.** Connect three large rings with two small rings. The large rings lie flat; the small rings stick up. This is the first row of large rings and the first row of small rings **(FIGURE 1)**.
**2.** Place a closed large ring over each of the two small rings. Do not go through any rings. The small rings will be sticking up through the middle of the large closed rings. This is the second large-ring row **(FIGURE 2)**.

In all subsequent rows, large rings will always go through small rings—and vice versa.

**3.** Slide a large ring through the two small rings added in step 1 **(FIGURE 3)**.

**4.** Slide a large ring through the outside of the first small ring. Slide a second large ring through the outside of the second small ring. This is the third large-ring row, and the beginning of the "one large-ring row followed by two small-ring rows" (L-S-S) pattern **(FIGURE 4)**.
**5.** Slide a small ring through the two large rings added in step 2 **(FIGURE 5)**.
**6.** Slide a small ring through the outside of one large ring and a second small ring through the outside of the other large ring from step 2. Be sure to keep this small-ring row behind the small rings added in step 1. This is the first small-jump-ring row in the (L-S-S) pattern **(FIGURE 6)**.
**7.** Slide a small ring through the two leftmost large rings of the three rings added in step 4. Slide a second small ring through the two rightmost large rings added in step 4. Be sure to keep this small-ring row behind the small rings added in step 6. This is the second

small-ring row in the (L-S-S) pattern **(FIGURE 7)**. Small-ring-rows alternate between two-rings wide and three-rings wide **(FIGURE 8)**. Large-ring rows alternate in the same way.
**8.** Slide a large ring through the leftmost two small rings and around the small ring behind them. Add a second large ring through the rightmost two small rings and around the small ring behind them. This is the beginning of the next L-S-S ring pattern **(FIGURE 9)**.

Even though the final dragonscale pattern presents as alternating large-ring and small-ring rows, it is made with a large-ring row followed by two small-ring rows.

**9.** Continue adding rows in the L-S-S pattern until you reach the desired length.

# EUROPEAN 4-IN-1

Ring sizes and the number of rows added give the European 4-in-1 chain very different looks. The sizes and row information for each project using European 4-in-1 can be found in the project's materials list.

**1.** Slide an open ring into two closed rings, and close the ring. Slide another open ring on the first ring, and close the ring. This creates a 2-in-1-in-1 chain **(FIGURE 1)**.
**2.** Hold the piece sideways to make it easier to connect new rings. Spread the two end rings open as shown. To add new rings, always position the side rings behind the center ring **(FIGURE 2)**. If the side rings are in front of the center ring when you add the next row, you are looking at the back of the piece and the weave will not work **(FIGURE 3)**.
**3.** To add the next row, slide an open ring down through the bottom ring and up through the top ring. This will be the new center ring. Don't close the ring **(FIGURE 4)**.
**4.** Slide a closed side ring onto the open center ring, and lay it out as shown **(FIGURE 5)**.
**5.** Slide a second closed side ring onto the open center ring, and lay it out as shown. Close the center ring **(FIGURE 6)**.
**6.** Repeat steps 2–5, adding open center rings and closed side rings, until you reach the desired length **(FIGURE 7)**.
**7.** To widen the rows, slide an open ring through two side rings on the finished chain, and close **(FIGURE 8)**.
**8.** Slide an open ring through the next two side rings, and close **(FIGURE 9)**. Continue to add new rings into the next two overlapping side rings down the entire side of the chain. When finished with one side, turn the chain over and add rings down the other side in the same manner.

**Figure 1**

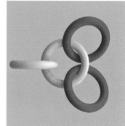
**Figure 2**

**Figure 3**

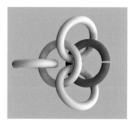
**Figure 4**

**Figure 5**

**Figure 6**

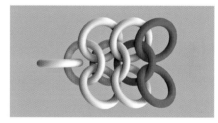
**Figure 7**

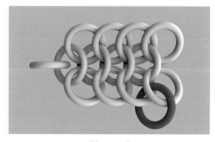
**Figure 8**

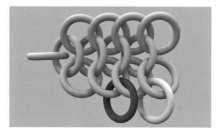
**Figure 9**

Figure 1

Figure 2

Figure 3

Figure 4

Figure 5

Figure 6

Figure 7

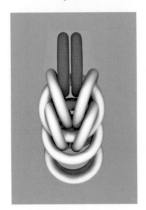

Figure 8

## FULL PERSIAN

**1.** Follow steps 1–5 of the Byzantine chain mail weave (p. 97).

**2.** Slide an open ring into the two rings added in step 5 of the Byzantine weave. Hold the open ring with your pliers so that you can see the "O" shape of the ring facing you **(FIGURE 1)**.

**3.** Grasp the twist tie at the bottom of the weave, and raise it up and directly behind the chain until it sticks out horizontally from the open O ring held in your pliers. This will place the open ring right next to the wide end of the upside-down V formed by the two rings on the chain. Slip the open ring through the V, and close the ring **(FIGURE 2)**.

FIGURES 3–5 illustrate the path of the ring in step 2.

**4.** With that ring facing you, slide a new open ring into two rings next to and behind the ring you just added **(FIGURE 6)**. Keep the ring open, and repeat step 3 **(FIGURE 7)**.

**5.** Once you have both rings "flipped" to either side, spread two rings open to create a space. Insert two new rings into the space created **(FIGURE 8)**. Add open rings, and flip them into the wide ends of the V (steps 2 and 3).

**6.** Repeat step 5 until the chain is the desired length.

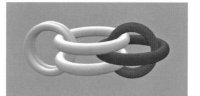

Figure 1          Figure 2          Figure 3

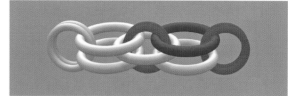

Figure 4          Figure 5

Figure 6          Figure 7

## HELM

Helm mail uses two ring sizes referred to in these directions as large and small. Rings are described as "sets of double large, single large, and double small" to set the stage for constructing helm flowers (p. 104).

**1.** Slide two large open rings into four small closed rings, and close the rings. Lay them out as shown **(FIGURE 1)**.

**2.** "Sandwich" a large ring between the previous set of double large rings and around the set of double small rings on the end **(FIGURE 2)**.

**3.** Slide an open large ring through the set of double small rings and beneath the single large ring added in step 2 **(FIGURE 3)**.

**4.** Slide a set of double small rings into the large ring added in step 3, and close the ring **(FIGURE 4)**.

**5.** Slide a second large open ring into the two sets of double small rings, making sure that it is above the large ring added in step 2, and close the ring **(FIGURE 5)**.

**6.** "Sandwich" a single large open ring between the previous double set of large rings and around the set of double small rings, and close the ring **(FIGURE 6)**.

**7.** Repeat steps 2-5 for the length of the project **(FIGURE 7)**.

**Figure 1**

**Figure 2**

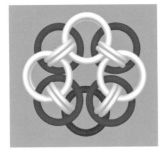

**Figure 3**

**Figure 4**

## HELM FLOWER

The helm flowers in this book are constructed with rings in different amounts and sizes. The number of rings in a flower is designated as "sets" of double large rings, single large rings, and sets of double small rings.

**1.** Start with a strip of helm chain with three sets of double large rings, four sets of single large rings, and four sets of double small rings (or as directed in the project).
**2.** Grasp the large single sandwiched rings from each end of the piece in step 1, and bend them around in a circle with the large single rings almost touching **(FIGURE 1)**.

**3.** Slide an open large ring into the two sets of small rings at the end of the helm strip, and close the ring. Make sure that the large ring lies in front of the end large rings **(FIGURE 2)**.
**4.** Turn the piece to the other side with the large ring added in step 3 behind the large rings on the end **(FIGURE 3)**.
**5.** Slide an open large ring into the same two sets of small rings, and close the ring. Make sure that the new large ring lies in front of the end large rings **(FIGURE 4)**.

## CLEO'S HELM

**1.** The large rings in standard helm mail follow a pattern of: single sandwiched ring, doubled rings, single sandwiched ring, doubled rings.
**2.** The pattern for Cleo's helm is: skip, replace, skip. Skip a sandwiched ring, replace a sandwiched ring with a diamond, and skip a sandwiched ring. Repeat this pattern for the desired length.

**Figure 1**

**Figure 2**

**Figure 3**

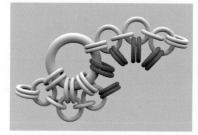

**Figure 4**

**Figure 5**

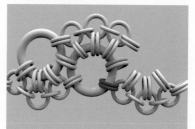

**Figure 6**

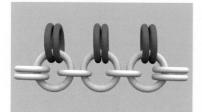

**Figure 7**

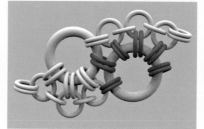

**Figure 8**

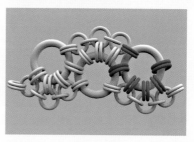

**Figure 9**

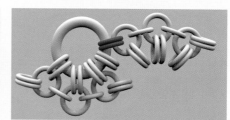

**Figure 10**

## SCALLOP

**1.** Open four small rings and close six small rings. Slide an open ring through three closed rings, and close the ring. Slide a second open ring through the same three closed rings, and close the ring. Make two of these 3-in-2 chain pieces. Lay them out like a two 2-in-2-in-1 chain **(FIGURE 1)**.

**2.** Connect the two chains with two small rings sliding through the single rings from each 2-2-1 chain to make a base chain **(FIGURE 2)**.

**3.** Make the required number of these base chains **(FIGURE 3)**.

**4.** Slide two small rings into a middle pair of rings in the base chain. Repeat for the two remaining pairs of rings **(FIGURE 4)**. Repeat for all the other base chains.

**5.** Slide a large ring into the three two-ring sets added in step 4; add two more small rings, and close the ring **(FIGURE 5)**.

**6.** Pick up another base chain from step 4, and turn it upside down.

**7.** Re-open the large ring, slide it into the leftmost two rings from the end of the upside-down base chain, and close the ring **(FIGURE 6)**.

**8.** A new large ring will slide through the path of rings as shown in **FIGURE 7**.

The two rings added in step 5 don't line up with the other rings in the path.

**9.** Slide a large ring through the two-ring set from the previous base chain, the two rings added in step 5, and the three two-ring sets of the current upside-down base chain. Add two more small rings, and close the ring **(FIGURE 8)**.

Snug the large ring over to include the tight connection of the two-ring set.

**10.** Pick up another base chain from step 4, and hold it right side up. Re-open the large ring, slide it into the leftmost two rings at the end of the current base chain, and close the ring **(FIGURE 9)**.

**11.** Slide a new large ring through the two-ring set from the previous base chain, the two small rings, and the three two-rings sets from the current right side up base chain. Add two small closed rings, and close the ring **(FIGURE 10)**.

**12.** Repeat steps 9-11, alternating upside-down and right-side-up base chains, for the desired length.

Figure 1

Figure 2

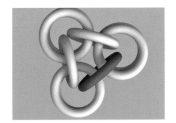

Figure 3

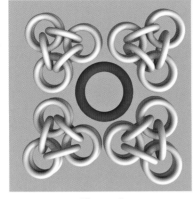

Figure 4

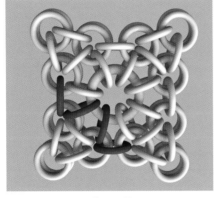

Figure 5

Figure 6

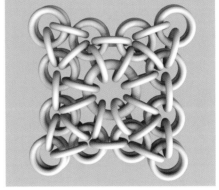

Figure 7

Figure 8

## VICTORIAN LACE

**1.** Open two small rings and close six small rings (you will be working with small rings in steps 1-4). Slide an open ring through four closed rings, and close. Lay out the chain with two rings to the left and two rings to the right **(FIGURE 1)**.

**2.** Slide the remaining open ring through two closed rings, and connect to the two rings on one end of the chain **(FIGURE 2)**.

**3.** Slide an open ring through the two closed rings on both sides of the chain, and close the ring to

form a triangle **(FIGURE 3)**.

**4.** Repeat steps 1 and 2 three times.

**5.** Close a large ring. Place the four triangles around the large ring **(FIGURE 4)**.

**6.** Using small rings, connect the top two triangles to each other with a single ring through the two-ring points on each triangle. Then connect each triangle end-point to the large ring in the center **(FIGURE 5)**.

**7.** Continue connecting the remaining triangles to each other

and to the large ring. You may find it easier to connect the triangles to each other before connecting them to the large ring in the center. An alternative method is to first connect all the triangles to the large ring and then to each other **(FIGURES 6 AND 7)**.

**8.** Repeat steps 4-7 for the desired number of lace squares **(FIGURE 8)**.

# Wire Techniques

## HOOKS

Hooks are used to grab and connect, and are frequently compressed to take up the minimum amount of space. While they start out looking a lot like loops, their job includes becoming one with the design lines.

Use the roundnose pliers' tips to catch just the very end of a wire. Turn the pliers to wrap halfway around the tip. Make interlocking hooks to end or connect wires by threading the crook of one through the other. Use flatnose pliers to compress first one hook and then the other.

## LOOPS

Use chainnose pliers or the very tip of roundnose pliers to bend the wire at a right angle to the tail. Slide the jaw of the roundnose pliers forward to determine the size of the loop needed. Position the jaws with the bend centered. Bring the wire over the top of the pliers' jaws and around until it meets the bend. Trim the wire just to touch.

### UNWRAPPED LOOP

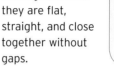

**1.** Using the roundnose pliers' tips to bend the wire at a right angle.
**2.** Slide the top jaw forward to determine the size of the loop needed. Position the jaws with the bend centered. Bring the wire over the top of the pliers' jaw.
**3.** Reposition the pliers vertically so the lower jaw fits snugly in the loop. Curve the wire around the bottom jaw of the roundnose pliers.
**4.** Use the pliers' tips to bend the wire away from the loop at a right angle.

### WRAPPING A LOOP

Position the end of a wrapping wire at the back of the loop base, leaving a tail. Bring the working end from behind, and wrap this wire over the front of the loop base and around to the back. Make as many wraps as needed, and trim the tail and working wire. Press the cut ends close to the loop base.

## BINDING

In the projects for this book, compound elements are bound together with half-round wire using the following wire-wrap technique:

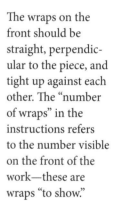

**1.** Lay out the wires to be bound, making sure that they are flat, straight, and close together without gaps.
**2.** Tape the wires to prevent shifting.
**3.** Use flush-cut pliers to cut a piece of half-round wire at least 3" (7.6cm) long. Use flatnose pliers to make a hook in the wire. Carefully bend the hook off-center, and create a slant away from the direction in which you will be wrapping.
**4.** Position the bent hook over the wire bundle so the short nose of the hook is at the back or inside of the work. Use flatnose pliers to compress the hook. The working wire should be at the front of the piece and perpendicular to it. Gently push the working wire toward the back and then up using your thumb or index finger. Make the wrap as snug as you can. Compress this part of the wrap with flatnose pliers.
**5.** Use your index finger or thumb to press the wire over the top and down the front to make a snug wrap. Use flatnose pliers to compress this turn and complete one wrap.
**6.** Repeat for the number of wraps indicated in the instructions. Compress as you go.

The wraps on the front should be straight, perpendicular to the piece, and tight up against each other. The "number of wraps" in the instructions refers to the number visible on the front of the work—these are wraps "to show."

**7.** Pull the final working end of the wrapping wire away from the back of the piece. Clip the wire with a flush cutter. Use flatnose pliers to press the end back into place.

When all the wraps are in place, you can still adjust them slightly. Then use flatnose pliers to do a final compression and tighten the wrap.

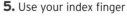

## OVERCAST STITCH

To bind wires together with an overcast stitch, use fine wire (28-30 gauge). Leave a 1" (2.5cm) tail, and bring the working end of the wire across the front of the wires to be bound. Continue down the back. Bring the working end back to the front. Repeat.

## COILS

### COIL LOOP

Wrap a single wire around a specific spot on a roundnose pliers' jaw or around a dowel to produce a forward-facing loop. Repeat as needed to make the desired number of loops. Use this technique to create rings as well (cut the loops apart with wire cutters).

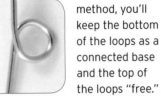

### SIDE-BY-SIDE COIL LOOPS

A row of coil loops can be shaped differently by pulling more or less in various directions. Start with a hollow coil.

**1.** Orient the coil so the coil loop ends are at the base of the formed loops (and pulling on the working wire will help complete the loop, not pull it open). With this method, you'll keep the bottom of the loops as a connected base and the top of the loops "free."

**2.** Push on the side of the coil to flatten it, and use nylon-jaw pliers to form the loops. Use your fingers for fine gauges. Pull the coil longer horizontally and flatten it, and repeat.

**3.** Pull each end of the row in a horizontal direction. The chain of loops will first become overlapped coil loops that are slightly oval.

**4.** Additional pulling in a horizontal direction will cause the loops to be less overlapped. This can increase the space between loops and reduce the width of the loops until you form a series of nearly closed loops.

**5.** If you pull in a slightly curved upward direction, the space between loops will increase, and the loop will stay rounder and get smaller.

### GRADUATED LOOPS

**1.** To make a series of loops graduated in size from large to small, wrap the working wire around the tapered jaw of round-nose pliers, a pencil point, or a sharpened dowel. Orient the coil so the coil loop ends are at the base of the formed loop (and pulling on the working wire will help complete the loop, not pull it open).

The more tapered the cone, the more dramatic the change in the size of the loops will be.

**2.** Push on the side of the coil to flatten it and form the loops. Use your fingers for finer gauges, and use nylon-jaw pliers for thicker gauges. Alternate pulling the coil longer horizontally with flattening the coil.

Continue until you reach the desired amount of overlap or loop shape. The row of loops will be graduated in size.

To help make multiple pieces uniform, mark or tape the pliers' jaw and use the top edge of the tape as the beginning wrap point. Make the same number of wraps each time.

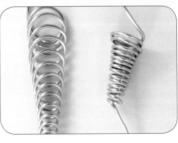

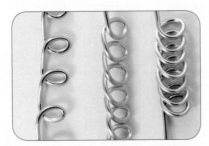

## CLASP HOOK

**1.** Begin with a wire extension as directed in the project. Compress the extended wires, and make sure that they are flat and parallel. On the front of the piece, use roundnose pliers to bend the tip of the wire extension up **(PHOTO A)**.

**2.** Turn the piece over. Catch the tip of the hook with one jaw of the roundnose pliers. Place the other jaw at a point halfway along the extension. Use the pliers to roll the wires over and form a hook **(PHOTOS B AND C)**.

# Resources

**Beadalon Artistic Wire**
440 Highlands Blvd.
Coatesville, PA 19320
www.beadalon.com

**Gill Mechanical Company**
3604 W. 4th Ave. #B,
Eugene, OR 97402
www.tubewringer.com

**Swanstrom Tools**
3300 James Day Ave.
Superior, WI 54880
www.swanstromtools.com

**Paramount Wire Co. & CBC Metal Supply**
2-8 Central Ave.
East Orange, NJ 07018
www.parawire.com

**Rio Grande**
7500 Bluewater Rd. N.W.
Albuquerque, NM 87121
www.riogrande.com

**Fire Mountain Gems and Beads, Inc.**
One Fire Mountain Way
Grants Pass, OR 97526
www.firemountaingems.com

**Urbanmaille (for chain mail rings)**
68 Lazy Lane
Pine, CO 80470
urbanmaille.com

# From the Authors

## ACKNOWLEDGMENTS

The path of writing a book starts with an inquisitiveness about how to create what you see, either physically or in the mind's eye. The next step is to explore for the sheer joy of it. The directions take form when someone else asks to be shown what you did and how you did it. Our thanks goes to the students, who are so enthused, so curious, and so interested. They have been the true marvels throughout this process. We set out to capture the designs and techniques in this book for them and ended up learning a lot ourselves.

We would like to thank a few other people who helped to make this book a reality.

Wilfred Traeger: You made the photos possible. We do hope that you like your new camera a lot, as this one is staying here.

Bill Freundlich and Dale (Cougar) Armstrong: You are wonderful and patient wire-wrapping teachers. Just look at where that has led.

Kerry Bogart: You shared and helped so much, and we didn't even buy you coffee—yet.

Lucy Setiz: When you said a final piece was something you would enjoy wearing, we knew it was classic.

Hollis Heinzerling: Things stayed in focus because of your generosity.

David G. DeYoung: There aren't enough thanks in the world for your patient instruction in the world of 3D images. We couldn't have done it without you!

Marilynne Lipshutz: You and Studio 34 in Rochester have helped launch the careers of so many budding artists.

Authors Guild: Thank you for always being in the authors' corner.

A special "unlimited minutes" thank you goes to our editor, Erica Swanson, and marketing gurus, Linda Franzblau, Jami Rinehart, and Janice Zimdars, for their supportive communication through the publication process.

To my husband Frank, who can "pull a rabbit out of the hat" every time, when magic is required to fix the computer or get the ideal parking place. You have been my best helper and cheering section — Karen

To my husband and helpmate David, who lent an ear and a shoulder during the two long years of writing this book — Barbara

## AUTHOR BIOGRAPHIES

Karen Rakoski

Karen Rakoski is a designer, artist, and author who enjoys working with fibers, silver, glass, gems, and wire materials. Her jewelry projects have been published in magazines such as **Art Jewelry**, **Bead&Button**, and **Step by Step Wire Jewelry**, and featured in the books **30 Minute Earrings** and **30 Minute Rings**. She has won awards at the local and international levels for her jewelry designs and creations. She teaches both children and adults through classes, writing, and videos. Born in the Midwest, she now lives with her husband and two cats in upstate New York, where she continues to create and share her ideas.

Barbara DeYoung

Barbara DeYoung is an artist and a jewelry designer, but foremost, she is a teacher. She is a senior instructor at Rochester's Studio 34 Learning Arts Center and also teaches her repertoire of bead weaving, chain mail, and wire wrapping classes in local schools, libraries, and bead stores. One of the founding members of Upstate New York Bead and Glass Guild, Barbara served as its program director for many years. She has also won awards for her chain mail designs from the Rochester Lapidary Society.

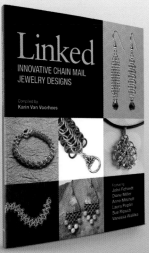

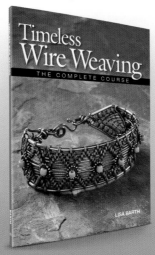
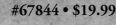